MY FIRST PIANO
Adventure®
FOR THE YOUNG BEGINNER
by Nancy and Randall Faber

Hello! I'm Tap, the music firefly.
Look for me throughout the book!

NOAh

This book belongs to:

Progress Chart

Friends at the Piano

Hi! It's me, TAP. Your friends from Book A are back with two famous composers from l - o - n - g ago. Let's meet them!

1. This is WOLFGANG AMADEUS MOZART.
   Practice saying his name with your teacher!

Mozart

Millie

Marta

Carlos

A composer is a person who writes music.

FF1621

2. This is LUDWIG VAN BEETHOVEN.
   Practice saying his name with your teacher!

3. Listen to the CD and point to
   the friends and composers as
   they are named.

Beethoven

Mrs. Razzle-Dazzle

Katie

Dallas

♩ By the way, can you find Tap
   on this page?

Parade of Friends
Review of Book A

Tip from Tap:

Follow the directions above each flag.

Play and name.

Name. How many beats?

Dallas

Play and name.

Beethoven

Name. What do these mean?

f *p*

Mrs. Razzle-Dazzle

Play and name.

Carlos

Play and name.

Tap

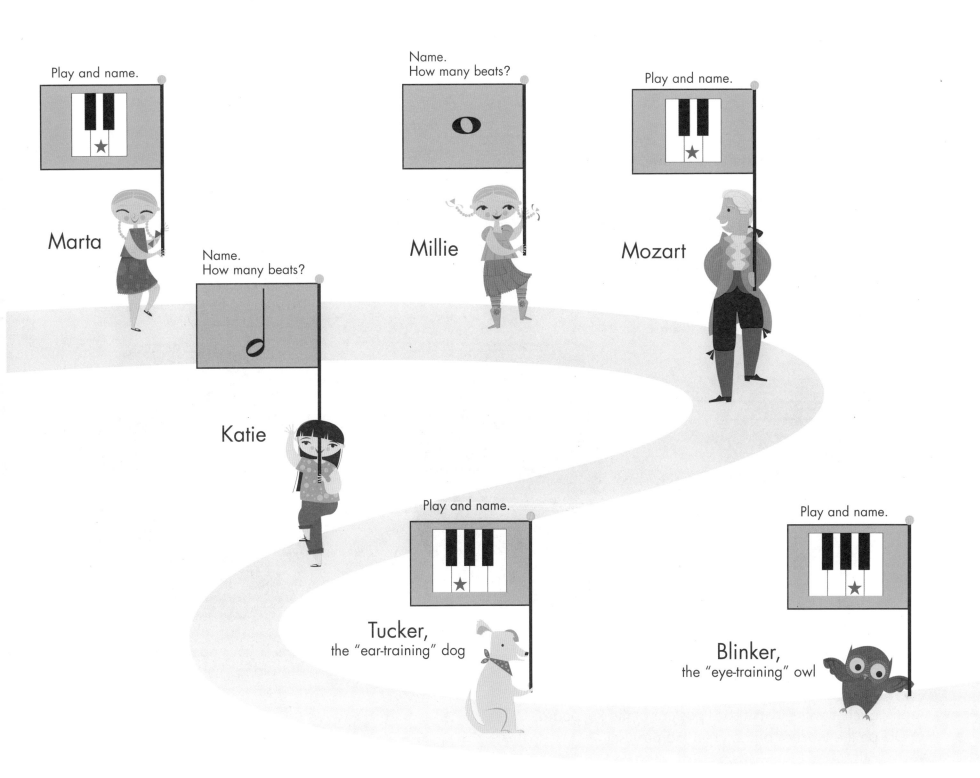

Play and name.

Marta

Name.
How many beats?

Katie

Name.
How many beats?

Millie

Play and name.

Mozart

Play and name.

Tucker,
the "ear-training" dog

Play and name.

Blinker,
the "eye-training" owl

Posture Power
Review: Seating Position

Tips from Tap:
These warm-ups can begin your lessons or practice!

1. Arm Circles

Swing your arms in a big s-l-o-w circle.

Feel as if you've swung your shoulders back and hung them on a coat rack!

2. The "I'm Great" Pose

Sit tall on the front half of the bench. With arms straight, your knuckles should reach the fallboard.

3. Ready to Play

Now rest your hands gently on the keys. Your arms should be level with the keyboard. Are you sitting tall yet relaxed?

Note: If you have to lean, move the bench forward or backward.

This is your position for playing the piano.

CREATIVE Your teacher will sit with poor posture at the keyboard. YOU be the teacher and correct the posture!

♩ Tap fell asleep. Can you find him?

Making Glasses
Review: Finger Numbers, Hand Position

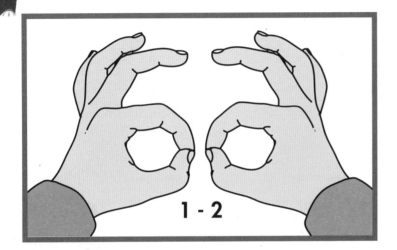

1. Make glasses with **fingers 1** and **2** and look through them.

2. Now set them down on the closed keyboard, balancing on the fingertips.
Do you have a **round hand shape**?

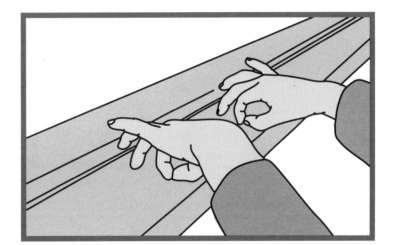

3. Repeat the above warm-up with these fingers.

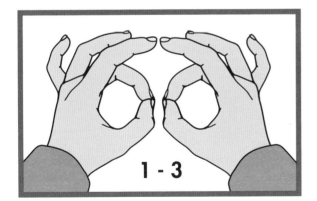

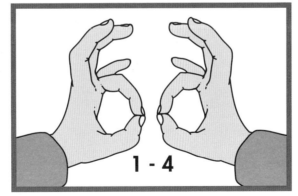

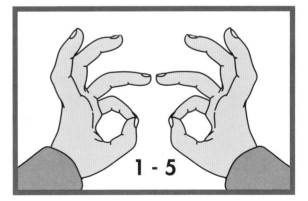

DISCOVERY Your teacher will ask to see your "glasses".
How fast can you form the ones that are called?

Tips from Millie and Marta:

1. Tap the rhythm of the song as your teacher plays **Duet 1, 2,** then **3**.

2. Play and say finger numbers, letter names, or words.

3. When you are ready, let your "pony" *walk, trot,* and *gallop* with the duets.

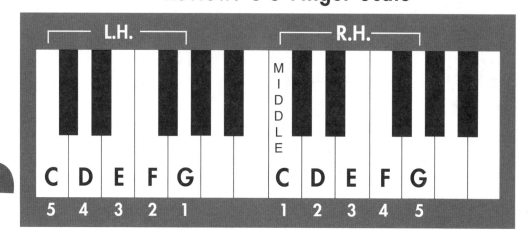

2 Giddy-up, Pony!

Review: C 5-Finger Scale

L.H. C D E F G — 5 4 3 2 1
R.H. C D E F G — 1 2 3 4 5
MIDDLE

Traditional words

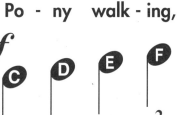  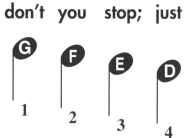 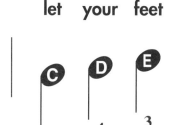 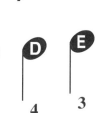 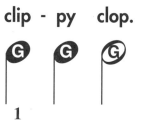

Po - ny walk - ing, don't you stop; just let your feet go clip - py clop.

𝄢 *f*

C D E F | G F E D | C D E F | G G G

L.H. 5 4 3 2   1 2 3 4   5 4 3 2   1

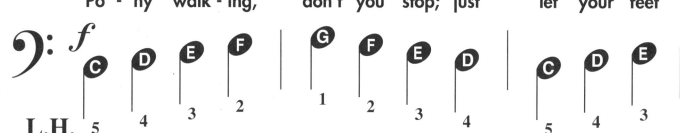

First Week Teacher Duet: *Pony Walk* (Student plays *1 octave higher* on the keys.)

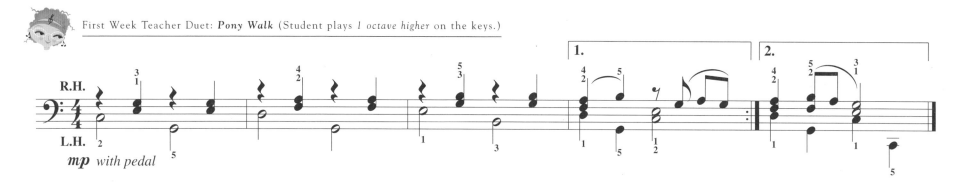

R.H.

𝄢 4/4

L.H.

mp with pedal

Repeat 2 more times
for *Pony Trot*
and *Pony Gallop.*

5 *measure number*

R.H.

Tail goes swish and   wheels go round, now   gid - dy up; you're   home-ward bound!

Second Week Teacher Duet: **Pony Trot** (Student plays *1 octave higher* on the keys.)

Third Week Teacher Duet: **Pony Gallop** (Student plays *1 octave higher* on the keys.)

A Note from Beethoven:

Long ago as I took afternoon walks, my fingers would *silently* play melodies that I compose.

Will you and your teacher play the game Silent Melody?

Silent Melody: (on the closed keyboard)

1. With rounded hands, *silently* play the melody with L.H. and then R.H. Say the finger numbers aloud.

At the keyboard:

2. Now play with firm fingertips. Create **forte** sounds!

TECHNIQUE GAME: Silent Melody

Ode to Joy
C 5-Finger Scale

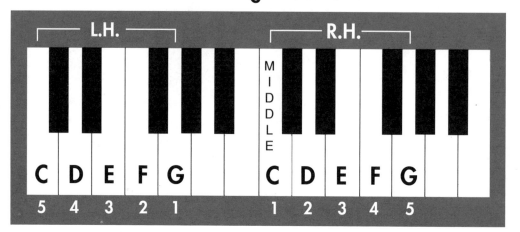

Ludwig van Beethoven
(Theme from the 9th Symphony)

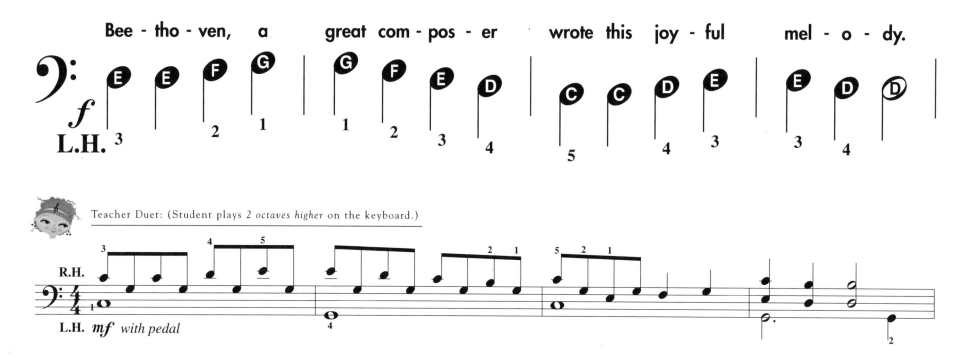

R.H.

3	4	5	5	4	3	2	1	2	3	2	1
E	E	F	G	G	F	E	D	C	C	D	E	D	C	C

Bee - tho - ven, a great com - pos - er wrote this theme for you and me.

DISCOVERY

Can you memorize *Ode to Joy?*

The Grand Staff

A staff has **5** lines and **4** spaces. Piano music uses TWO staffs. Together they form the **GRAND STAFF**.

1. Count the **lines.** Count the **spaces.**
   Now point to the line or space your teacher calls!

For the bass clef, count
from the **top** to the **bottom.**

R

L

2. For fun, listen to the *Grand Staff Song* on the CD often.
   It will introduce you to the grand staff.

♩ Where's Tap?

Music Alphabet on the Grand Staff

1. The music alphabet, **A B C D E F G,** can be written *3 times* on the grand staff. Can you find and circle the music alphabet 3 times below?

2. Brace **R.H. finger 3** with the thumb.
Play *Middle C* and all the keys HIGHER to the top of the keyboard. These are **treble notes**.

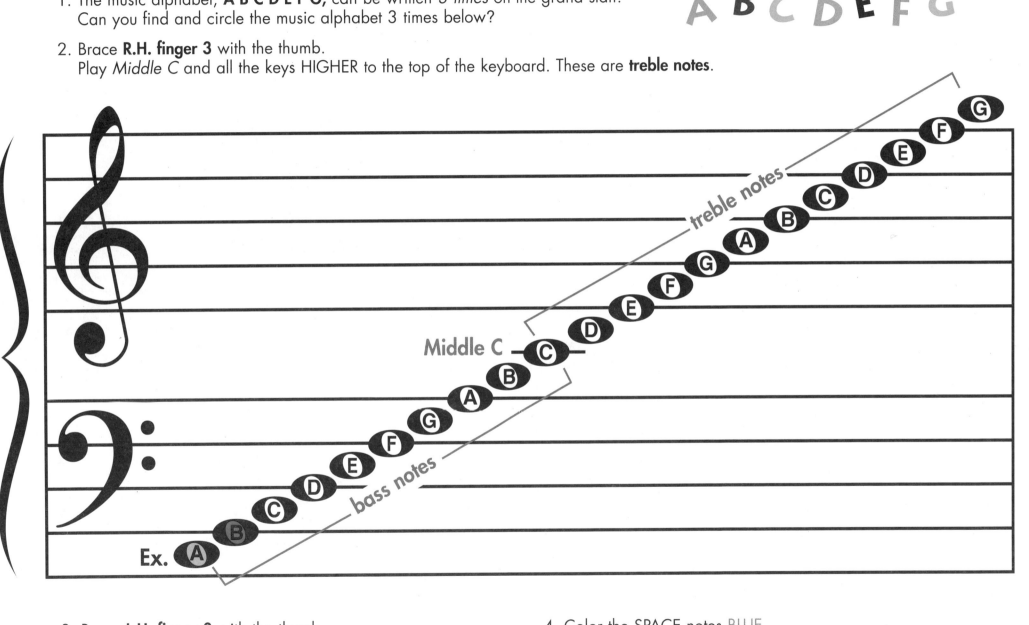

3. Brace **L.H. finger 3** with the thumb.
Play *Middle C* and all the keys LOWER to the bottom of the piano. These are **bass notes**.

4. Color the SPACE notes BLUE.
Color the LINE notes RED.

Middle C for Bass Clef

Pretend the bass clef is the King.
Can you find the two buttons popping off his chest?

The king has a cat named **Middle C Cat**.
Find the "whisker" line in the face of Middle C Cat on the throne.

Tips from King Bass Clef:

1. Make Middle C Cat "purr" by gently tickling the
   Middle C key with **L.H. finger 2**, then **3**, then **1**.

2. Now watch your teacher play the piece. Your turn!
   Make Middle C Cat jump to your thumb at the end.

5 **The King's Cat**

Repeat **p** *(piano)*.

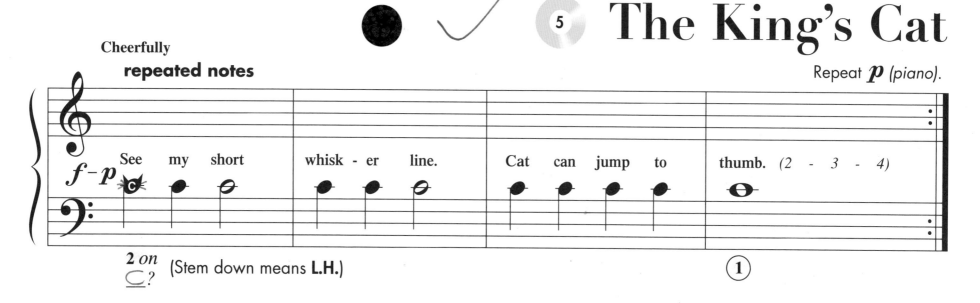

Cheerfully

repeated notes

f–p See my short | whisk - er line. | Cat can jump to | thumb. *(2 - 3 - 4)*

2 *on*
☞? (Stem down means **L.H.**)

①

DISCOVERY Can you play this piece beginning with the **L.H. finger 3**?
Jump to your thumb once again for the *last* note.

Middle C for Treble Clef

Pretend the treble clef is the Queen with a long swirly dress.
The Queen also adores her cat, **Middle C**.

Tips from Queen Treble Clef:

1. Make Middle C Cat "purr" by gently tickling the
   Middle C key with **R.H. finger 2**, then **3**, then **1**.

2. Now watch your teacher play the piece. Your turn!
   Make Middle C Cat jump to your thumb at the end.

The Queen's Cat

Happily

2 *on*
C? (Stem up means **R.H.**)

① Repeat *p* (piano).

f - p See my short whisk - er line. Cat can jump to thumb. *(2 - 3 - 4)*

Create your own **Middle C Melody** with the teacher duet.
Try changing to different fingers as you play!

Teacher Duet for pp. 18–19 (Student plays *as written*.)

R.H.

mf - pp

Treble Clef D

Treble D looks a little like Middle C—except there's no whisker! Is D a LINE or SPACE note?

MIDDLE

C **D**

Tips from Katie:

1. Your teacher will make up a rhythm(s) on **treble clef D**. Copy it back. Now do one for your teacher.

2. Play the piece. Sing letter names, then words.

to play with CD

Tub Time!

Brightly   **repeated notes**

1   2

1-2

p

Tuck - er   dog,   where   are   you?   You're   hid - ing   from   me.   Woof!

Prepare **L.H. finger 3** on the **LOWEST F**.

Play the LOWEST F on the piano.

f F
3

5 Circle the **repeated notes** to the end.

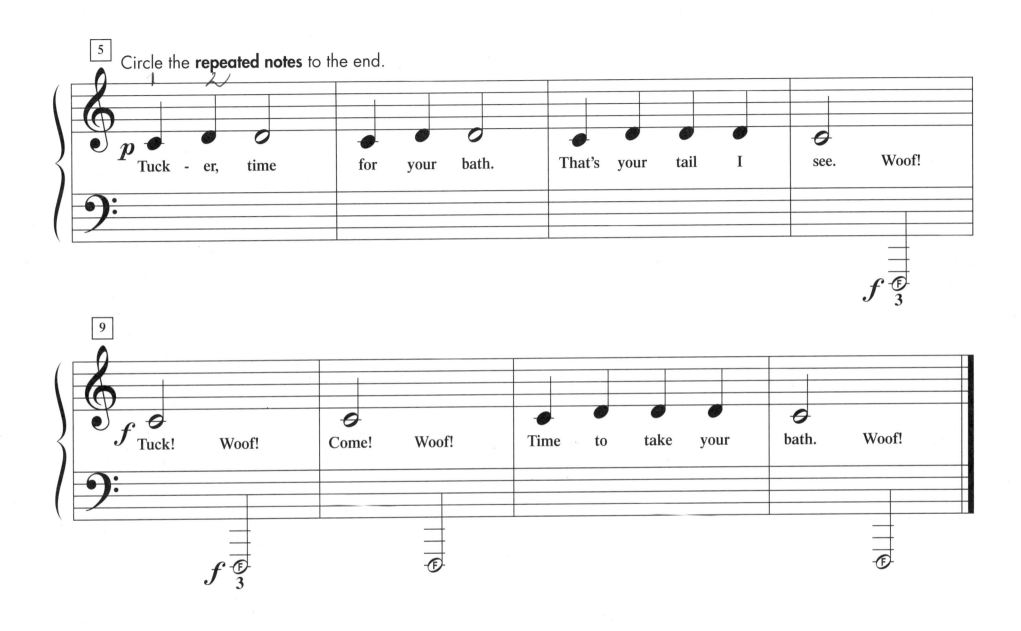

Tuck - er, time for your bath. That's your tail I see. Woof!

9

Tuck! Woof! Come! Woof! Time to take your bath. Woof!

DISCOVERY Now play *Tub Time* using **R.H. fingers 2** and **3** on Middle C and D keys.
Note: R.H. finger 2 will start on Middle C.

Steps on the Staff

To step, play the NEXT key up or down on the piano.

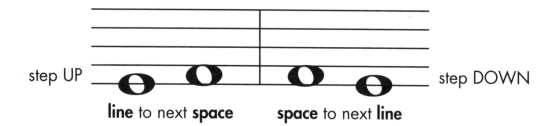

step UP

line to next **space**   **space** to next **line**

step DOWN

Tips from a goldfish:

1. Tap and count the piece aloud with your teacher.

2. For an underwater sound, your teacher may hold the **damper pedal** down throughout. Now you try!

to play with CD ✓

Gliding Goldfish

Gliding

Play loudly—the brightly colored fish is close to you!

1 *on* C ?

f Gold - fish,   gold - fish,   glid - ing   through   the   wa -   ter.

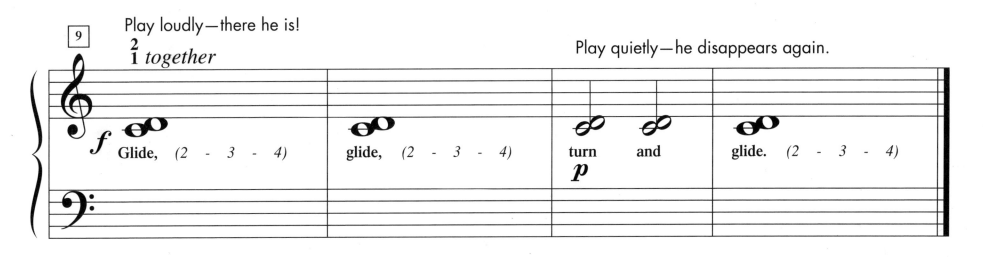

5 Play quietly—the fish disappears behind the coral.

p Gold - fish, gold - fish, glid - ing through the wa - ter.

9 Play loudly—there he is!

$\frac{2}{1}$ *together*

Play quietly—he disappears again.

f Glide, (2 - 3 - 4) glide, (2 - 3 - 4) turn and glide. (2 - 3 - 4)

p

DISCOVERY Can you play the piece again using **R.H. fingers 2-3** on Middle C and D keys?
Using **R.H. fingers 3-4**?

Teacher Duet: *8va* throughout (Student plays *as written.*)

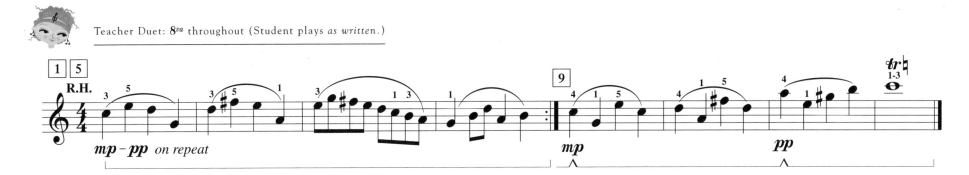

15

R.H.

mp - pp on repeat   *mp*   *pp*

Treble Clef E

Treble E sits on **line 1** of the treble staff.

Tips from Carlos:

1. Copy the rhythm your teacher plays on **E**. Now you be the teacher!

2. Play and sing letter names, th...

Pumpkin Party

Happily

1   2   3   echo!

f Or - ange lights,   *p* hap - py sights,   *f* pump - kins shin - ing   bright. (2 - 3 - 4)

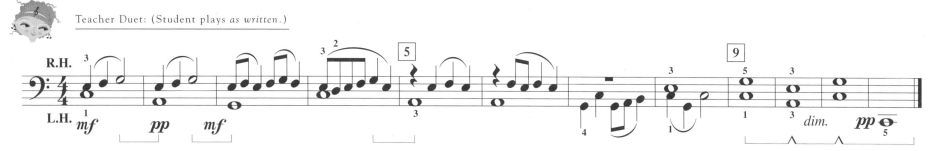

Teacher Duet: (Student plays *as written*.)

R.H. *mf*   *pp*   *mf*   L.H.   dim.   *pp*

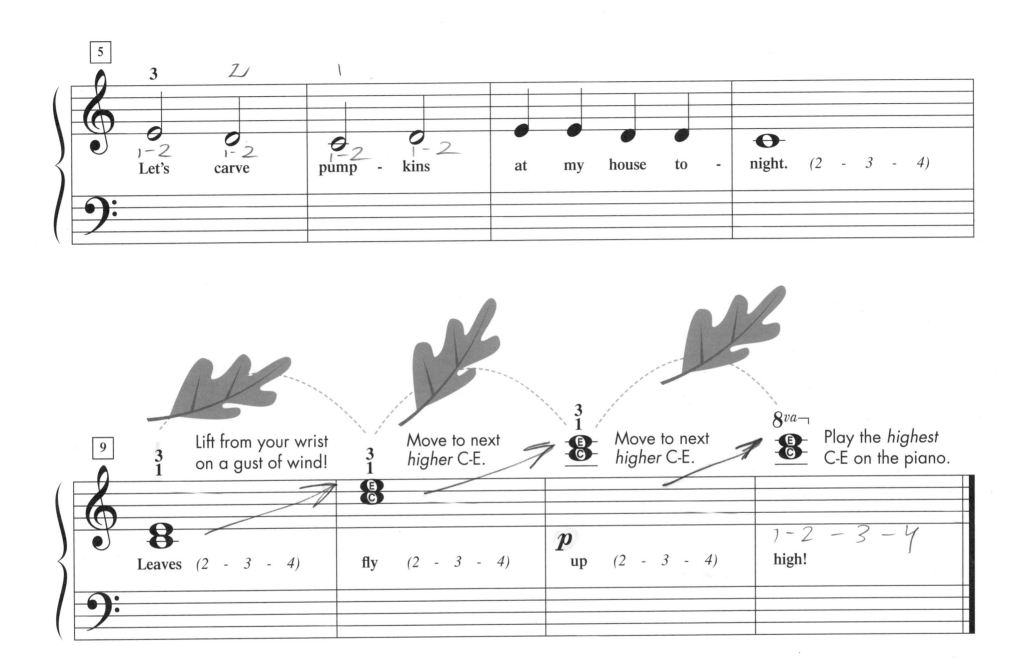

DISCOVERY

Point out 6 measures with **whole notes**.
Point out 2 measures with only **half notes**.
Point out 2 measures with only **quarter notes**.

Can you spot Tap at the party?

A Note from Mozart:

I love puzzles, arithmetic, and composing **musical patterns**.
A musician often memorizes a musical pattern.

Patterns by Memory:

1. First play each pattern looking at the notes.

2. Repeat and play each pattern by MEMORY on the next higher C-D-E. Watch your fingers to check your round hand shape!

3. Your teacher will play the first measure of any pattern. Point to the pattern you heard. Then YOU be the teacher.

Mozart's Musical Patterns

Quickly — pattern 1 — repeat — repeat

1.

p Come here quick - ly, come here quick - ly, come here quick - ly, please! *(2 - 3 - 4)*

Repeat on the next HIGHER C-D-E.

Teacher Duet: (Student plays *as written.*)

Pattern 1   Pattern 2   Pattern 3

H. W.

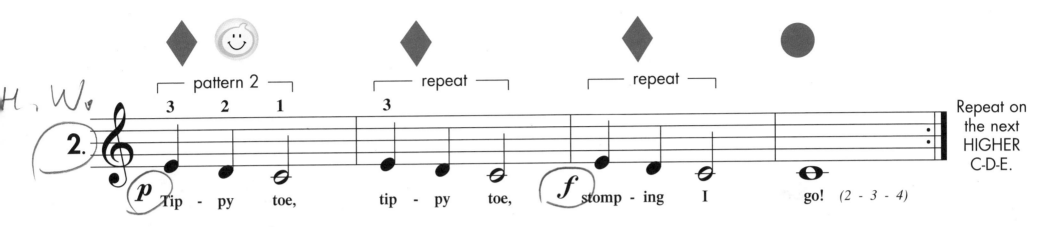

2.

pattern 2 | repeat | repeat

3 2 1   3

p Tip - py toe,   tip - py toe,   *f* stomp - ing I   go! *(2 - 3 - 4)*

Repeat on
the next
HIGHER
C-D-E.

Keep fingertips firm!

Way to GO!

3.

pattern 3 | repeat

1   3   1

f Mo - zart   sound, *(2 - 3 - 4)* *p* all   a - round. *(2 - 3 - 4)*

Repeat on
the next
HIGHER
C-D-E.

C R E A T I V E Make up your own short **C-D-E pattern**.
Then repeat your pattern on HIGHER C-D-E keys.

Bass Clef A

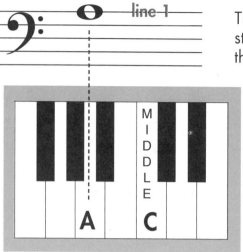

line 1

The TOP line of the bass clef staff is the first letter of the alphabet—**A**!

A — MIDDLE C

Tips from Dallas:

1. Copy the rhythm your teacher plays on **bass clef A**. Then reverse.

2. Play and count aloud, "1 1, 1-2," etc.

11

Ride the "A" Train

Cheerfully

Repeat using **finger 3**.

f All a - board,

p tick - ets please!

f A Train's leav - ing

now!

2 on A?

Teacher Duet: (Student plays *as written.*)

mf ⁵₁   *pp*   *mf*

FF1621

Tip from the Tooth Fairy:

The melody in *measures 1* and *2* appears two more times. Show your teacher.

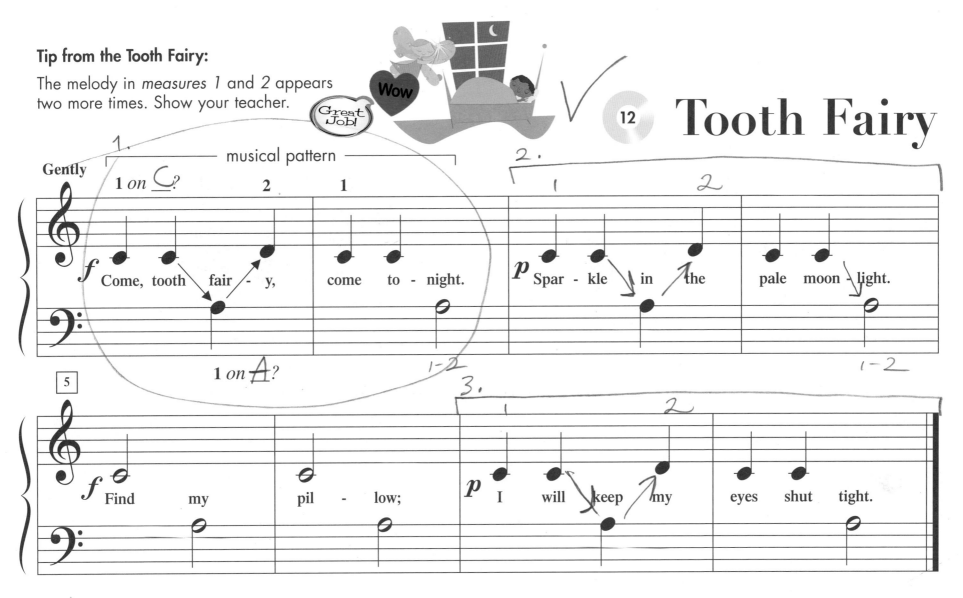

Tooth Fairy

Gently

f Come, tooth fair - y, come to - night.

p Spar - kle in the pale moon - light.

f Find my pil - low;

p I will keep my eyes shut tight.

DISCOVERY Choose a *different* L.H. finger for the **bass clef A** and play the song again.

Teacher Duet: 8va throughout (Student plays *as written.*)

✏️ | WRITING BOOK 24

NEW:

mf *(mezzo forte)* means moderately loud.
Your teacher will help you pronounce these words.

Choose any key and play it ***f***, then ***p***, then ***mf***.

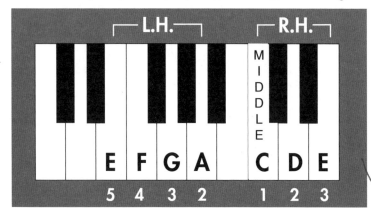

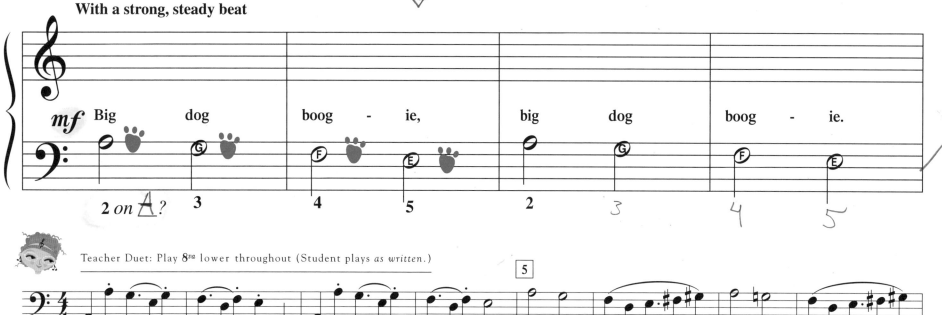

Great PLAY!

Yeah

13

Tucker's Secret Life

With a strong, steady beat

mf Big dog boog – ie, big dog boog – ie.

2 *on* A?   3   4   5   2   3   4   5

Teacher Duet: Play *8va* lower throughout (Student plays *as written.*)

8va lower throughout

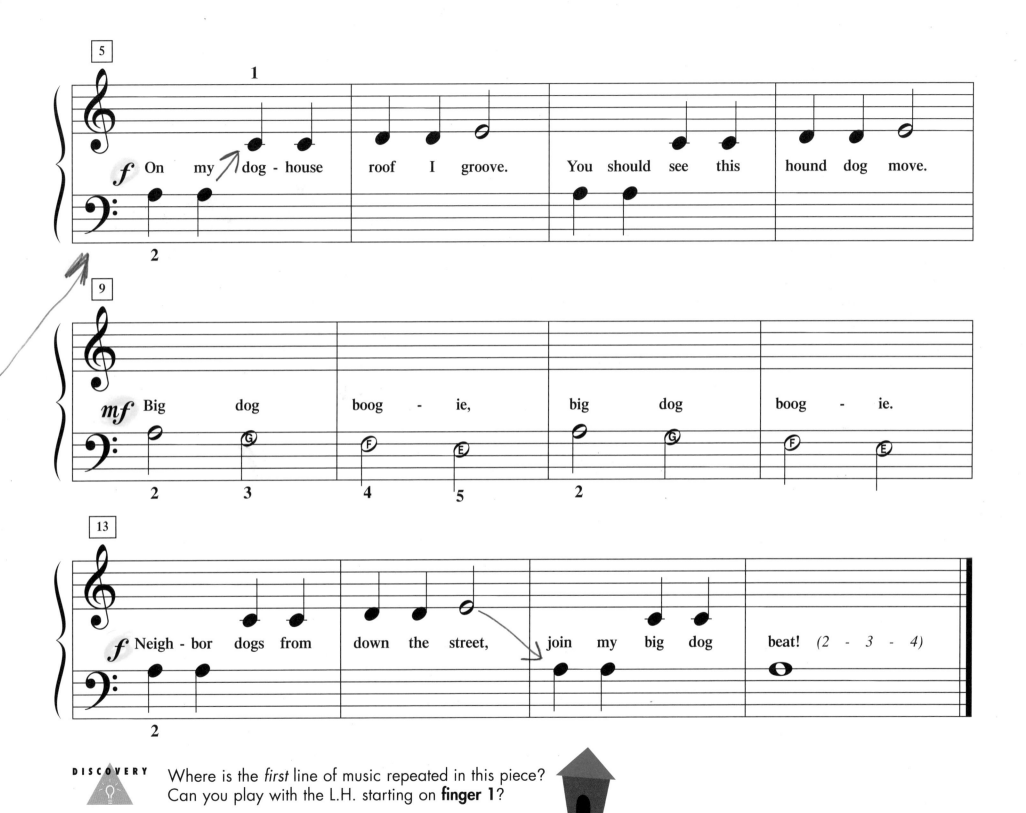

DISCOVERY Where is the *first* line of music repeated in this piece?
Can you play with the L.H. starting on **finger 1**?

Bass Clef B

B sits on top of the bass staff.
Is it a LINE or ~~SPACE~~ note?

Tips from Tap:

1. Tap and count the rhythm aloud with your teacher.

2. Play on firm fingertips with a great, steady beat!

14

A-B Bop!

Lively

mf | A | is | the | top | line. | Step | up | to | B. | *(2 - 3 - 4)* | Play 2 times!

3 *on* A?   1-2   1-2   ②

1-2

Teacher Duet: (Student plays *as written*.)

mf

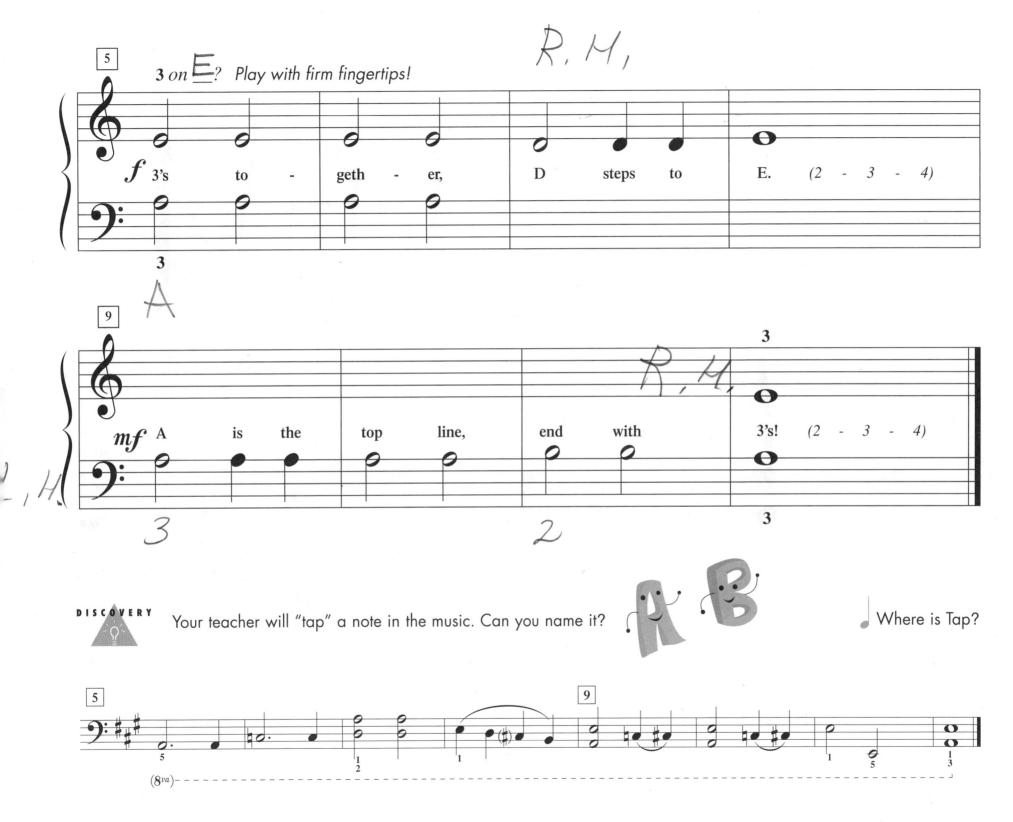

Your teacher will "tap" a note in the music. Can you name it?

Where is Tap?

The Dotted Half Note = 3 beats

count: **1 - 2 - 3**

draw   draw

1 - 2 - 3

Tips from Mrs. Razzle-Dazzle:

1. Play the notes above on any key. Count **1-2-3**.

2. Tap the rhythm of the piece as your teacher plays the duet.

3. The children dance without looking at their feet. Can you play without looking at your hands?

15 **Russian Folk Dance**

Traditional

Rather fast tempo

3 on E ?

f Lit - tle chil - dren | danc - ing 'round the | birch tree.

(prepare L.H.)

Think: A is the top line. Step up to _____ ?   1 on B ?   2 A   Repeat

Teacher Duet: (Student plays *1 octave higher.*)

R.H.

L.H.

mf

✏️ | WRITING BOOK **28-29**

A Note from Beethoven:

I love sudden changes from **forte** to **piano**!

$\boldsymbol{f}$ and $\boldsymbol{p}$ **Fingers:**

1. First, play each line of music *forte*. Sink to the bottom of the key on firm fingertips.

2. As you play *piano*, are your fingertips firm?

3. Circle Mr. Beethoven's $\boldsymbol{f}$ and $\boldsymbol{p}$ signs if your teacher heard your *forte* and *piano* fingers!

PATTERN 1: STEPPING DOWN

16 **Sounds of Beethoven**

Repeat playing $\boldsymbol{p}$.

Moderately

3 *on*
E ?

$\boldsymbol{f}$ Play   for - te,   please.   (2 - 3)   Deep   in   the   keys.   (2 - 3)
$\boldsymbol{p}$ Play   pian - o,   please.   (2 - 3)   Light   on   the   keys.   (2 - 3)

2 *on* B ?   Think: A is the top line. Step up to ___B___ ?   3

Teacher Duet: (Student plays *1 octave higher*.)

R.H.

L.H.

mf - *pp* *on repeat*

PATTERN 2: RIGHT - LEFT - LEFT

f *p*

3 *on* E?

Repeat playing ***p***.

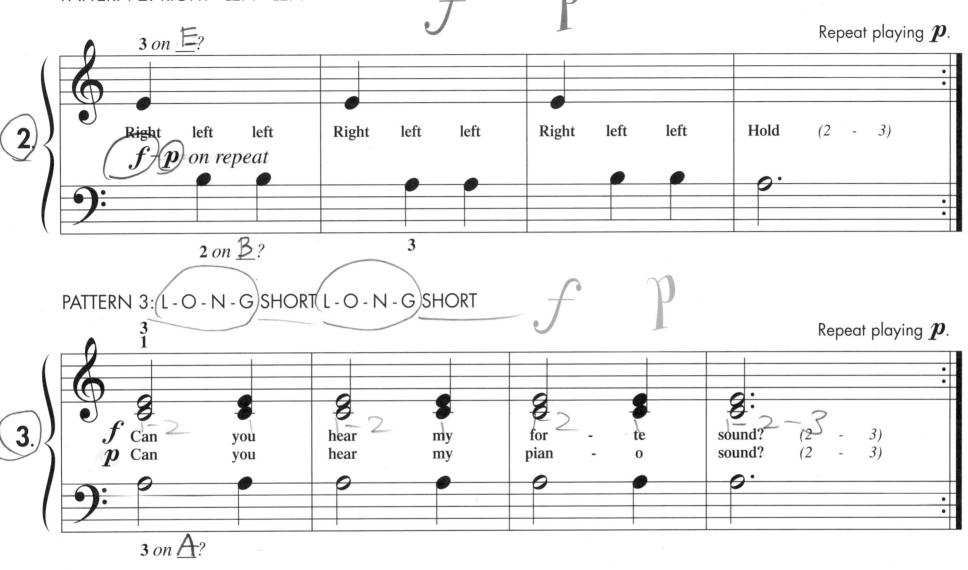

② *f* - *p* on repeat

| Right | left | left | Right | left | left | Right | left | left | Hold | (2 - 3) |

2 *on* B?

3

PATTERN 3: L - O - N - G SHORT L - O - N - G SHORT

f *p*

Repeat playing ***p***.

③ *f* Can you hear my for - te sound? (2 - 3)
   p Can you hear my pian - o sound? (2 - 3)

3 *on* A?

Teacher Duet: (Student plays *1 octave higher*.)

mf*-*pp on repeat

Teacher Duet: (Student plays *1 octave higher*.)

mf*-*pp on repeat

Time Signature

The **time signature** is two numbers at the beginning of the music.

4 means **4 beats** in a measure

4 means the **quarter note** gets 1 beat

Draw your own time signature.

Hint: Turn the lower 4 into a **quarter note** to help you remember what it means.

Tip from Tap:

Write the number of beats below each note. Does each measure have a total of **4 beats**?

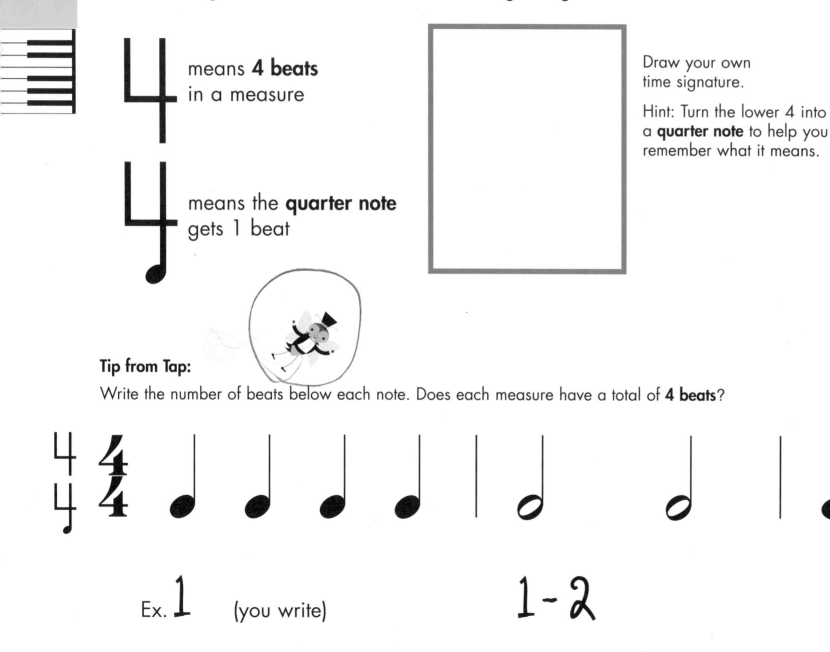

Ex. 1   (you write)   1-2

FF1621

the Time Keeper

_____
(your name)

1. Trace the first bar line.

2. Then draw a bar line after every **4 beats**.

3. Tap each rhythm **hands together** on the closed keyboard lid. Count aloud.

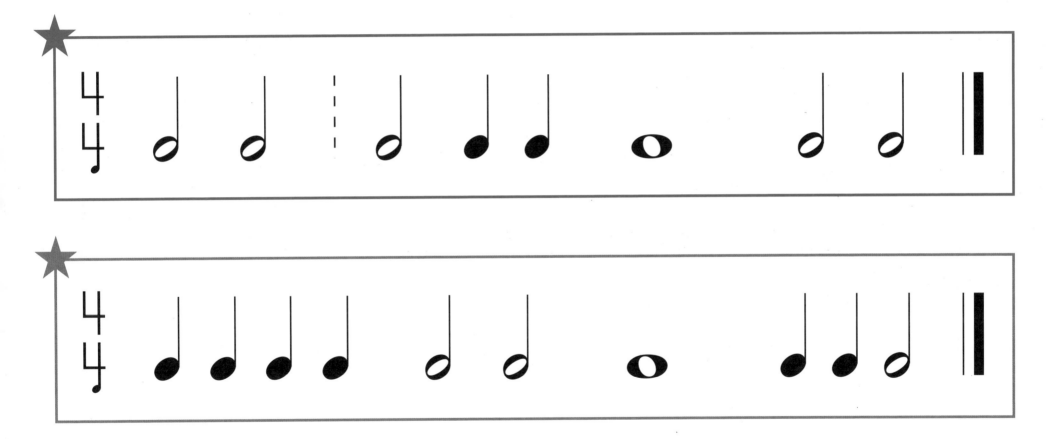

DISCOVERY Can you tap the rhythm in the RED box while your teacher taps the rhythm in the BLUE box? Then reverse!

Bass Clef G

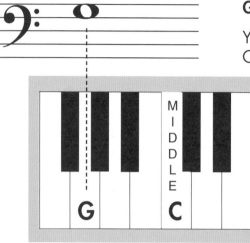

G sits on the *top space* just below top line A.

Your teacher will play a rhythm on **bass clef G**. Copy it back! Then reverse.

Tip from Millie and Marta:

On the **closed key cover**, tap and count the rhythm with your teacher. Be sure to tap with the correct hand!

17

Gallop, Pony

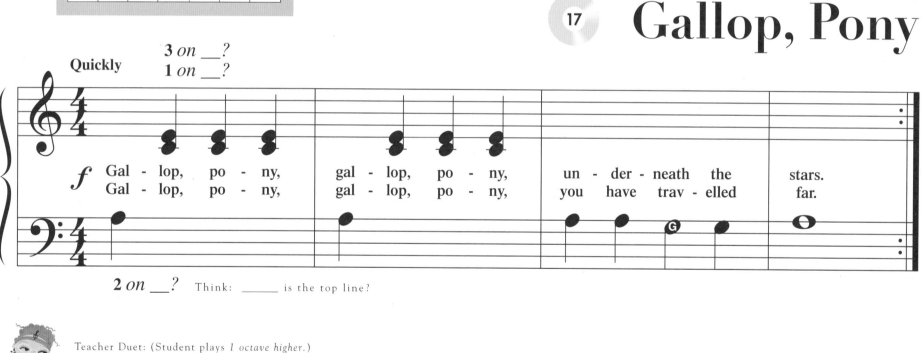

Quickly

3 *on* __?
1 *on* __?

f Gal - lop, po - ny,   gal - lop, po - ny,   un - der - neath the   stars.
Gal - lop, po - ny,   gal - lop, po - ny,   you have trav - elled   far.

2 *on* __?   Think: _____ is the top line?

Teacher Duet: (Student plays *1 octave higher*.)

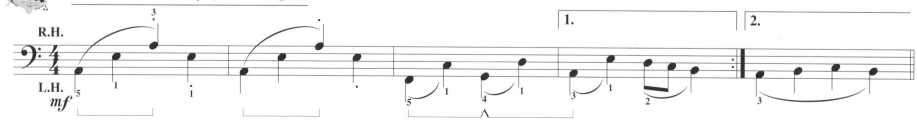

R.H.

L.H. *mf*

1.   2.

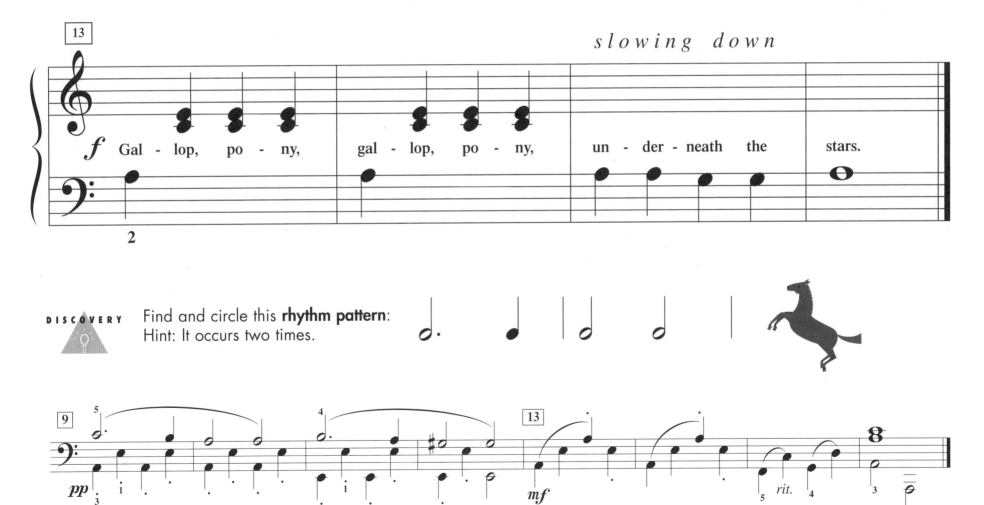

DISCOVERY Find and circle this **rhythm pattern**:
Hint: It occurs two times.

New Time Signature

3 means **3 beats** in a measure

4 means the **quarter note** gets 1 beat

18 King of the Land

Strong and proud

1 on __?

play ⅜ together

𝆑 King of the land! (2 - 3) King of the land! (2 - 3)

3 on __? Think: A is the top line. Step down to _____ ?

Teacher Duet: (Student plays *1 octave higher.*)

19 R.H. 5 13 1. 2.

L.H. 𝆐𝆑 5 with pedal 𝆐𝆏 rit.

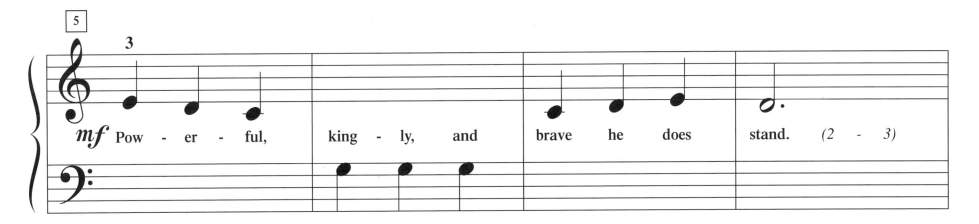

5 *mf* Pow - er - ful, king - ly, and brave he does stand. *(2 - 3)*

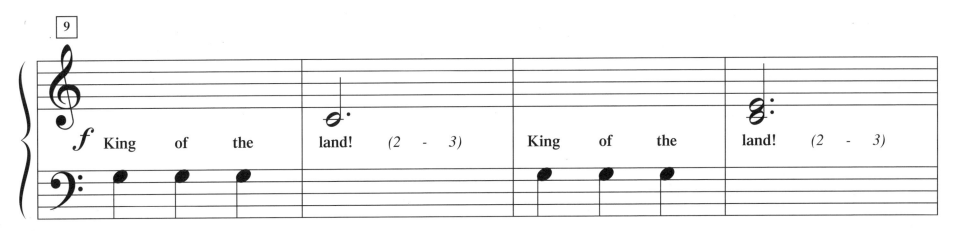

9 *f* King of the land! *(2 - 3)* King of the land! *(2 - 3)*

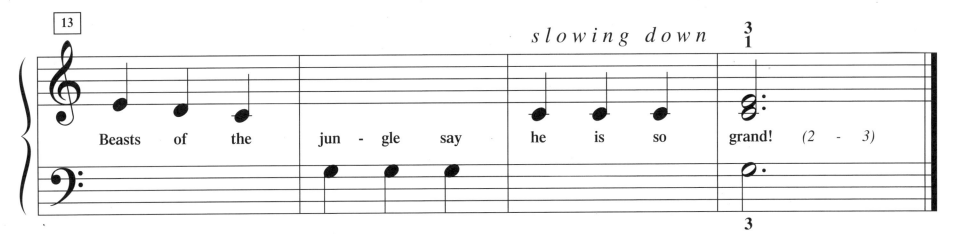

13 Beasts of the jun - gle say *slowing down* he is so grand! *(2 - 3)*

DISCOVERY

Where does the *first* line of music repeat later in this piece?

What is the *only* note that the L.H. plays for the entire piece?

Tips from Carlos:

1. Tap the rhythm wth the correct hand as your teacher plays the duet part.

2. Circle all the **repeated notes**.

3. Now play. Your teacher may sing the words.

19 # Tambourine Party

FF1621

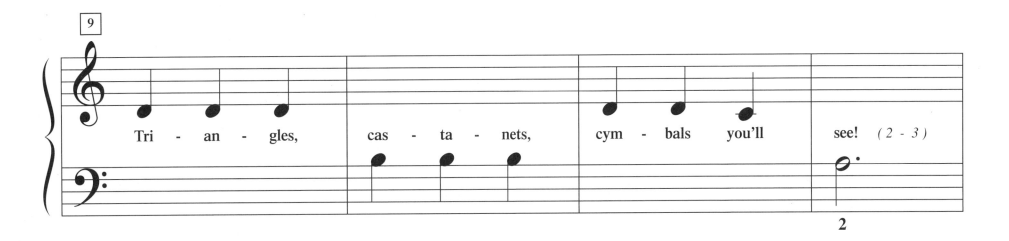

Tri - an - gles,   cas - ta - nets,   cym - bals you'll   see! *(2 - 3)*

2

3
f Wood blocks and   rhy - thm sticks   for you and   me! *(2 - 3)*

1

DISCOVERY Find these in your music:
the time signature, *mf* and *f* signs, bar line, double bar line

A Note from Mozart:

This melody is from one of my compositions for orchestra.
Each Finger Trick uses a *different fingering* for the same notes.

At the keyboard:

1. Practice **Finger Trick 1** and **2** until it's easy.

2. Tell your teacher which fingering you like better!

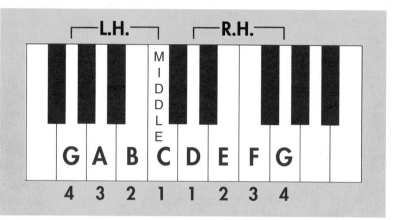

20 Finger Trick 1

Wolfgang Amadeus Mozart
(from Symphony in D, KV. 45)

arranged

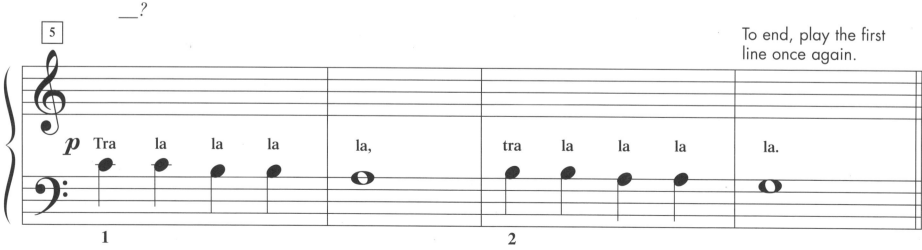

To end, play the first
line once again.

FF1621

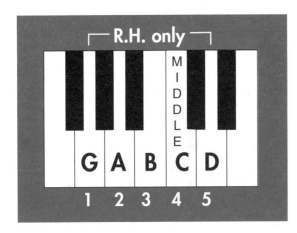

R.H. only

MIDDLE

G A B C D

1 2 3 4 5

Can you play Finger Trick 2
using only **R.H. fingers 1-2-3-4-5?**

2   *p*   4

TRA LA LA LA

1

f   3

Finger Trick 2

(for R.H. alone)

Quick and steady

I   can   change   the   fin - ger - ing   and   play   with   ease!
Play - ing   with   a   stead - y   beat   and   just   as   I   please.

5

Tra   la   la   la   la,   tra   la   la   la   la.

To end, play
the first line
once again.

CREATIVE Can you think of another fingering for your own **Finger Trick 3?**

Treble Clef F

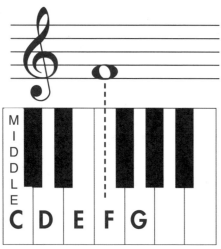

Tip from Tucker:

"Walk up" to the F and balance on a firm fingertip.
Your hand should be round like a scoop of ice cream!

21 # Ice Cream Dog

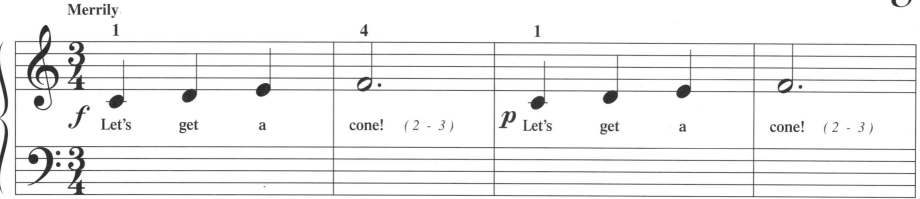

Merrily

Let's get a cone! (2 - 3)   Let's get a cone! (2 - 3)

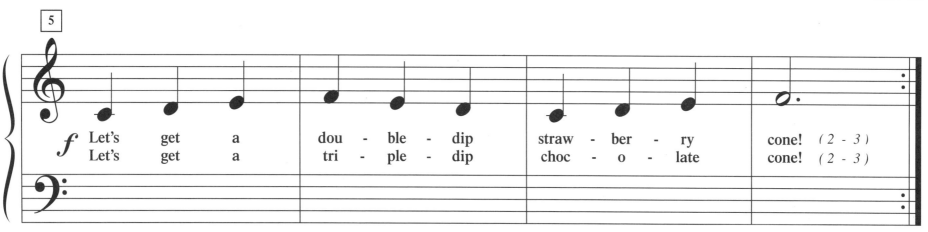

Let's get a dou - ble - dip straw - ber - ry cone! (2 - 3)
Let's get a tri - ple - dip choc - o - late cone! (2 - 3)

In this piece, create knocking sounds on the top of the fallboard.

Tips from Millie and Marta:

1. Practice the L.H. knocks in *measure 2.*
   Practice the R.H. knocks in *measure 6.*

2. Next, knock hands together in *measures 9–10.*

3. Now play. Have fun as you knock the piano!

22

Knock! Knock!

1

f Who's there? | Knock, knock, knock! | Who is knock-ing | at my door?

L.H. knocks fallboard

5 *R.H. knocks fallboard* | **9** *Both hands knock!*

Who's there? | Knock, knock, knock! | I just heard a | knock! | Knock! Knock! | Knock! Knock! Knock!

3 on
___?   Think: A is the top line. Step down to _____ ?

CREATIVE

Can you create your own hands-together knocking rhythm for the last *2 measures*?

Tips from a mocking bird:

1. First, tap the rhythm with your teacher.
   Count "1-2, 1 1, 1-2, 1-2, etc."

2. Next, circle all the **repeated notes** in the music.

3. Now play softly and slowly on firm fingertips!

A **lullaby** is a song to help someone go to sleep.

23 **Hush, Little Baby**

Traditional

Rather slowly

3 *on* ___ ?

p Hush, lit - tle ba - by, don't say a word, (2 - 3 - 4)
And if that mock - ing bird say will not sing, (2 - 3 - 4)

3 *on* ___ ?   Think: A is the top line. Step down to _____ ?

5

2

Pa - pa's going to buy you a mock - ing bird. (2 - 3 - 4)
Pa - pa's going to buy you a dia - mond ring. (2 - 3 - 4)

FF1621

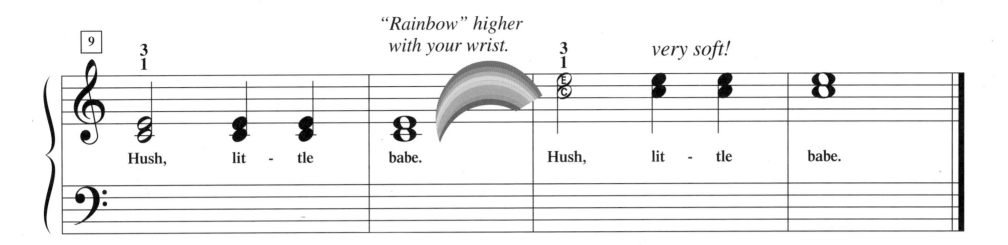

9

3
1

*"Rainbow" higher
with your wrist.*

3
1

very soft!

Hush, lit - tle babe. Hush, lit - tle babe.

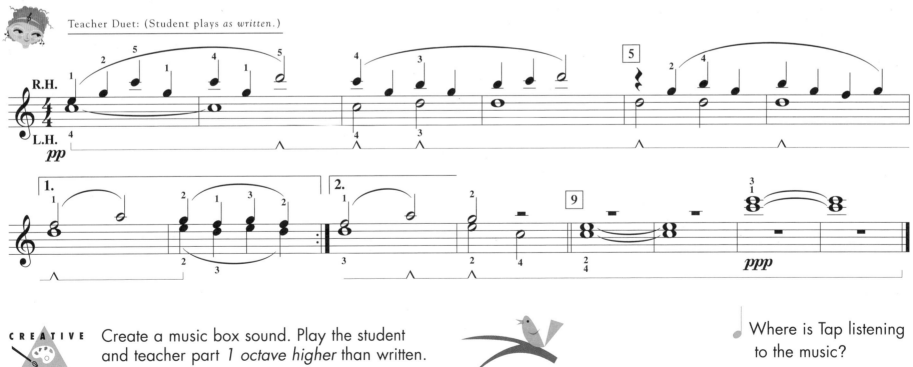

Teacher Duet: (Student plays *as written*.)

R.H.

L.H.

pp

5

1.   2.   9

ppp

CREATIVE Create a music box sound. Play the student
and teacher part *1 octave higher* than written.

♩ Where is Tap listening
to the music?

Tips from Mozart:

1. Can you and your teacher march in place with steady **half notes** to the CD?

2. Now play. Feel a strong march beat!

Wolfgang's Theme

Wolfgang Amadeus Mozart
(Theme from Variations K. 455)

Brisk march

1 *on* ___?

f Hear the drum - beat in the street. *(2 - 3 - 4)*

Think: A is the top line. Step up to _____ ? **1** *on* ___?

p Now the flute is play - ing gen - tle and sweet. *(2 - 3 - 4)*

Teacher Duet: (Student plays *1 octave higher.*)

R.H.

mf

L.H.

pp

Tips from Beethoven:

1. Circle all the **repeated notes**.

2. As you play, keep your eyes on the noteheads!

25

Ludwig's Theme

Ludwig van Beethoven
(from Symphony No. 7, Third Movement)

Walking briskly

When I'm walk - ing in the woods I hear tunes in my head. *(2 - 3)* Some -

Think: A is the top line. Step up to _____ ? **1** *on* __?

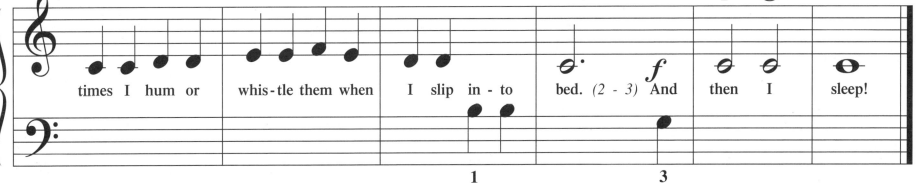

times I hum or whis-tle them when I slip in - to bed. *(2 - 3)* And then I sleep!

Teacher Duet: (Student plays *1 octave higher.*)

✏️ | WRITING BOOK **40-41**

A Note from Mrs. Razzle-Dazzle:

A baby learns to crawl before it learns to run.
I rode slowly on my bike before I raced down the street!

Play each melody with 3-Speed Fingers.

3-Speed Fingers:

1. S-L-O-W   You're learning to balance!

2. MEDIUM   Pick up the speed but keep it steady.

3. FAST   Hop on your fingertips and see how
             fast and steady you can go!

26

On My Two-Wheeler
(for LEFT HAND)

Fast and fun

mf

Repeat, beginning on
the next LOWER C.

Teacher Duet: (Student plays as written the first time, then *8va* LOWER for the repeat.)

mp

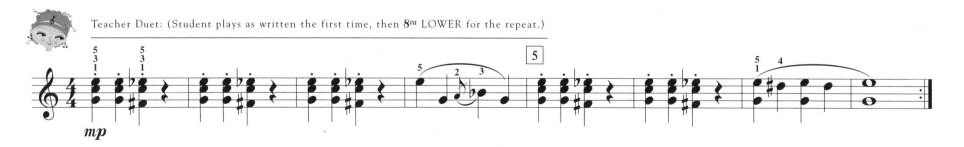

On My Two-Wheeler

(for RIGHT HAND)

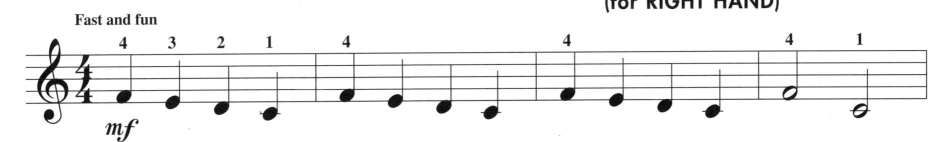

Fast and fun

mf

Repeat, beginning
on the next HIGHER F.

Teacher Duet: (Student plays as written the first time, then *8va* HIGHER for the repeat.)

Repeat 8va

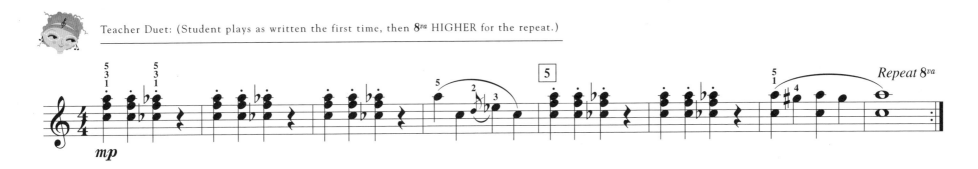

mp

Treble Clef G

1. Open your R.H. Pretend **fingers 1** and **5** are the wings of a plane. "Tip your wings" by rocking back and forth.

2. On the keyboard, use fingers 1 and 5 and rock between **Middle C** and **Treble G**.

3. On the staff, Treble G is written on LINE 2. Circle all the treble G's in *Airplane Pilot*.

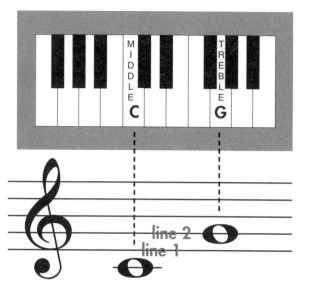

line 2
line 1

27 # Airplane Pilot

Flying quickly

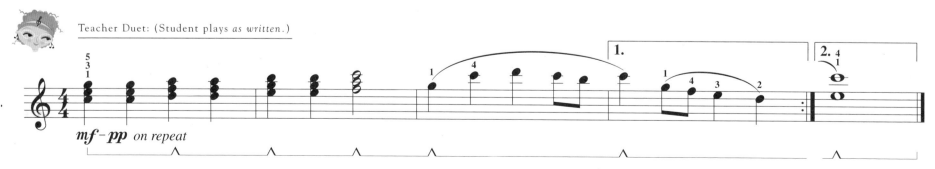

f Let your right hand   steer the plane   as you fly a - long. *(2 - 3 - 4)*
p Can you hold your   left arm straight   while you play this song? *(2 - 3 - 4)*

DISCOVERY Try this! As your R.H. plays, hold your left arm straight to the side, like an airplane wing!

Teacher Duet: (Student plays *as written*.)

mf - *pp* on repeat

Tips from Tap:

1. Find **Treble G** on the keyboard with **R.H. finger 2**. Put your R.H. back in your lap.

2. Do this again 3 times. How fast are you?

3. Now play. Hint: Singing the words may help you feel the rhythm.

28 # Tap, Be Nimble

Notice the new R.H. position. Finger 2 must balance on Treble G!

Lively

5

f Tap, be | nim - ble; | Tap, be | quick. | Tap's jump - ing | o - ver the
p Tap, be | quick and | Tap, be | fast. | Tap's jump - ing | o - ver it

2 on __?

9 *Slower*

can - dle - | stick. | Leap, | leap, | leap, | leap, | leap!
with a | dash! |

Play the HIGHEST C on the piano!

DISCOVERY Can you memorize this piece?

FF1621

29 Picnic with Friends

C 5-Finger Scale

Traditional words

Bright tempo

mf
I'm glad the sky is paint - ed blue, blue, blue.
Let's have a pic - nic; we can eat and play.

1 Think: A is the top line. Step down to _____ ?

Teacher Duet: (Student plays *1 octave higher*.)

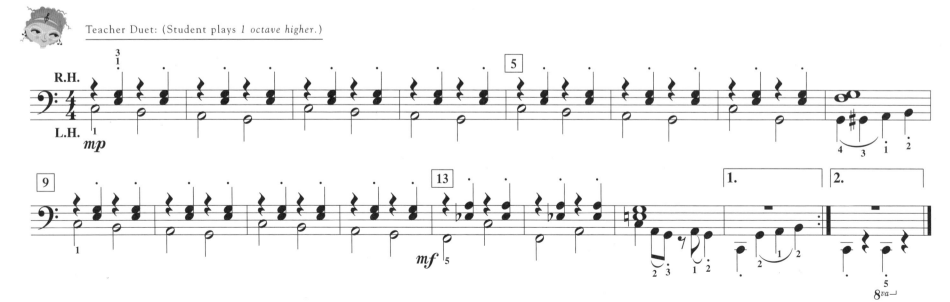

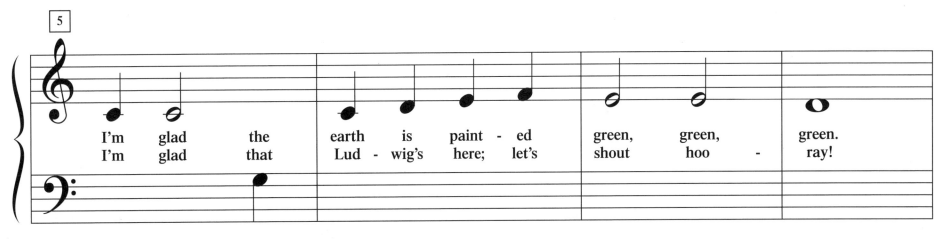

5

I'm glad the earth is paint - ed green, green, green.
I'm glad the that Lud - wig's here; let's shout hoo - ray!

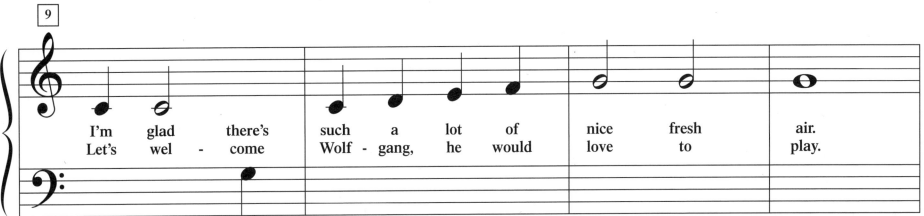

9

I'm glad there's such a lot of nice fresh air.
Let's wel - come Wolf - gang, he would love to play.

13

f I'm glad we're sand - wiched in be - tween. *p*
I'm glad my friends are here to stay!

Lift L.H. down $\frac{1}{5}$ to C-G.

DISCOVERY Tell your teacher what a **step** is on the keyboard and on the staff.
Then point out 3 measures that step in this piece.

Can you find Tap at the picnic?

A Note from Beethoven:

Pretend you have come to visit me.

Knocking Game: (on the closed keyboard)

1. Your teacher will knock the rhythm for *measures 1–2.* You answer by knocking *measures 3–4.* Knock your messages back and forth to the end of the piece.

At the keyboard:

2. Now play. Singing the words will help you feel the rhythm. Would Mr. Beethoven compliment your round hand shape?

TECHNIQUE GAME: Knocking Game

30 # Beethoven's Door

Ludwig van Beethoven
(from Bagatelle No. 1, Op. 33)

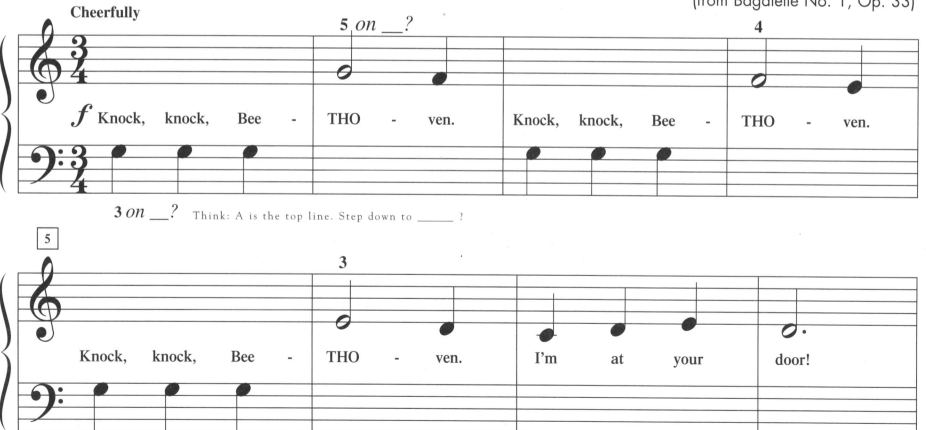

3 *on* __?   Think: A is the top line. Step down to _____ ?

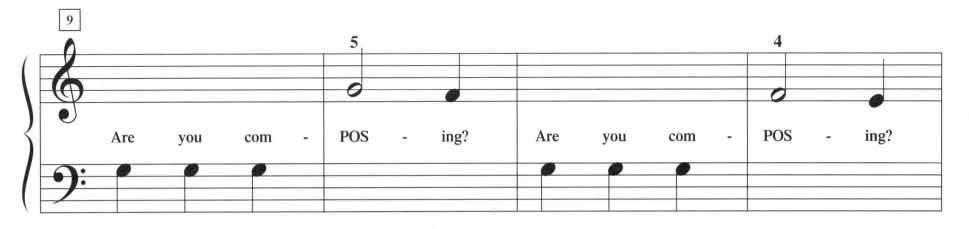

Are you com - POS - ing? Are you com - POS - ing?

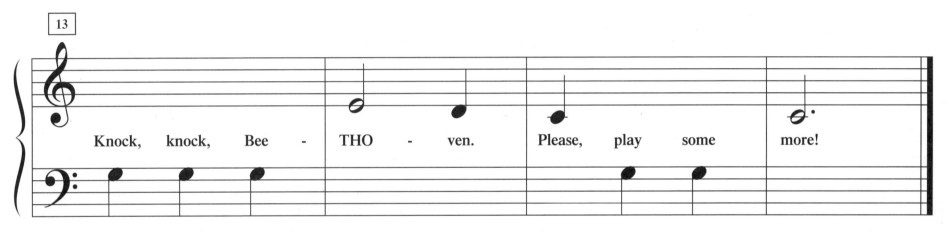

Knock, knock, Bee - THO - ven. Please, play some more!

DISCOVERY

Your teacher will *whisper* a L.H. finger number to you.
Play the piece again and use that finger to play **bass clef G**.

Teacher Duet: (Student plays *1 octave higher*.)

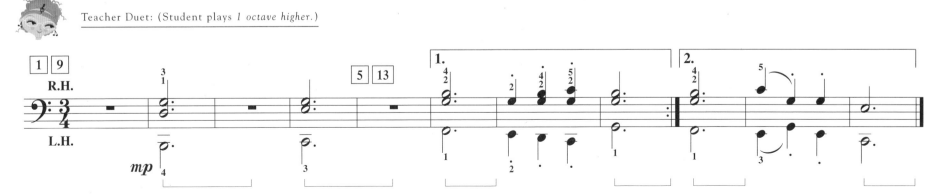

Bass Clef F

1. Open your L.H. Pretend **fingers 1** and **5** are wings of a plane. "Tip your wings" by rocking back and forth.

2. On the keyboard, use fingers 1 and 5 and rock between **Middle C** and **Bass F**.

3. On the staff, Bass F is LINE 2 going down. Circle all the Bass F's in this song.

31 Pilot, Land Your Plane

Lively

| | Pi - lot, | pi - lot, | land | your | plane | down | the | run - way, please. |
| | Pi - lot, | pi - lot, | land | your | plane, | wel - come | home | a - gain. |

mf

1 *on*
___?
5

1
5

DISCOVERY Try this. As your L.H. plays, hold your right arm straight to the side, like an airplane wing!

Teacher Duet: (Student plays *as written.*)

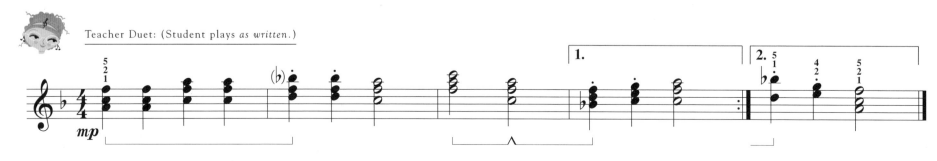

mp

1.   **2.**

Tips from Tap:

1. As your teacher plays the duet, "chime" the rhythm in the air with your arm. Pretend you are striking a gong!

2. Now play. For a big bell sound, hold the damper pedal down throughout the piece.

DING!
DONG!
DING!

32 Scotland Bells

Traditional

With joy

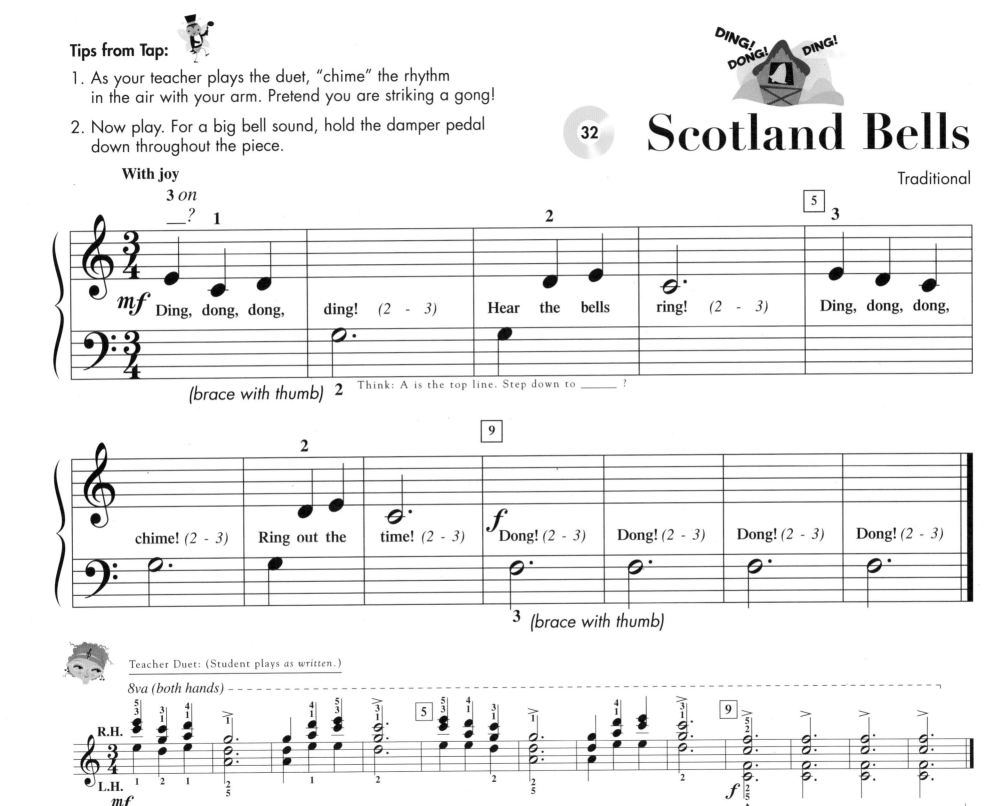

Teacher Duet: (Student plays *as written.*)

Dynamic marks

The loud and soft signs in music are called **dynamic marks**.
Your teacher will help you say this new musical term.

$$mf \quad f \quad p$$

1. Can you say the 3 dynamic marks above from:

   softest to *loudest* ?   *loudest* to *softest* ?

2. Circle each of these dynamic marks in your music.

33 I Would Like
to Go to Mars

Words by Crystal Bowman

Brightly

mf

I   would   like   to | go   to   Mars   and | zoom   past   all   the | stars.   *(2 - 3 - 4)*
Won - der what   I'd | see   as   I   ex - | plore   the   gal - ax - | y.   *(2 - 3 - 4)*

3 *on*

___ ?   Think: A is the top line. Can you finish the chant?

Teacher Duet: (Student plays *1 octave higher*.)

R.H.

L.H.   *mp*

mf

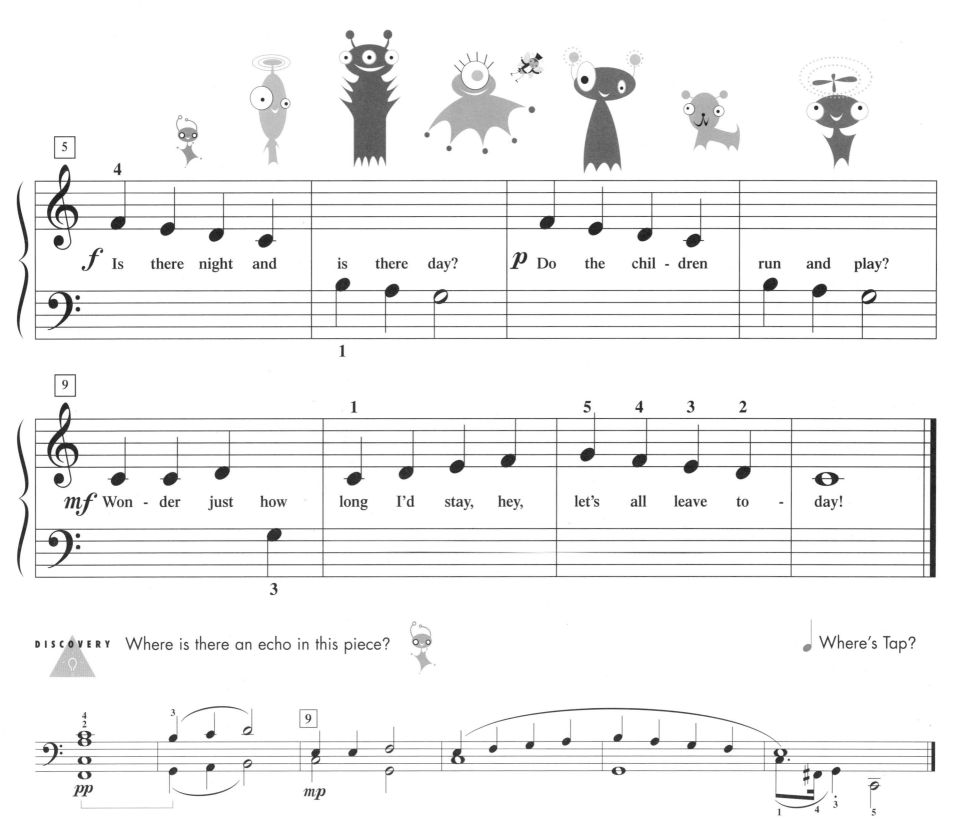

A Note from Katie:

Help the steam shovel dig LOWER into the ground!

Silent L.H. Jump:

1. Put your L.H. in the **starting position**. When your teacher says, "Jump," move down to the next LOWER C-F. Repeat, jumping LOWER again.

2. **Double Steam Shovel:** Play with the teacher duet. Move lower quickly so your steam shovels don't collide!

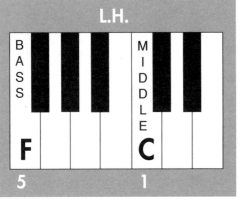

L.H.

BASS **F** 5   MIDDLE **C** 1

34 # Construction Zone

Steam Shovel (for L.H.)

Lively

Dig - ging down,   in   the   ground,   Dig,   dig   down!

PLAY 3 TIMES.
Move to the
next LOWER C
for each repeat.

mf   **1** *on* __?   **5** *on* __?   **1** **5**

Teacher Duet: (Student begins as written and moves **8**^{va} LOWER for each repeat.)

mp L.H.

A Note from Carlos:

Help steer the crane HIGHER into the air.

Silent R.H. Jump:

1. Put your R.H. in the **starting position**. When your teacher says, "jump," move up to the next HIGHER C-G. Repeat and jump HIGHER again.

2. **Two Cranes:** Play with the teacher duet. Keep your cranes moving steadily higher so they don't collide!

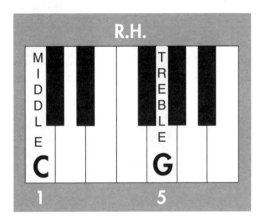

35 # Construction Zone

The Crane (for R.H.)

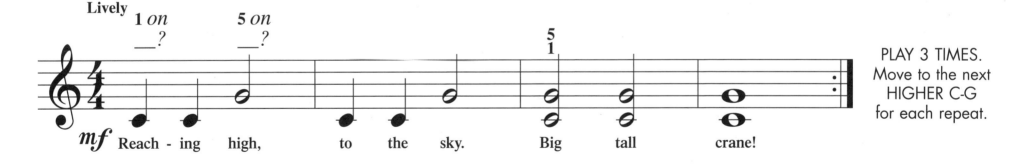

Lively

1 *on* __?   5 *on* __?

mf Reach - ing   high,   to   the   sky.   Big   tall   crane!

PLAY 3 TIMES.
Move to the next
HIGHER C-G
for each repeat.

Teacher Duet: (Student begins as written and moves **8**va HIGHER for each repeat.)

Bass Clef C

1. Play the first C *below* Middle C.
   This is called **Bass C**.

2. On the bass staff, the **3rd space down** is Bass C.
   Point to the top space and count down, saying,
   "1-2-3. The pearl is in the C."

3. Play the piece bracing L.H. finger 3 with the
   thumb—like a round shell.

4. At the end, turn your hand over and "open your shell."
   If you kept a good hand position, your teacher will lift
   out a pretend pearl.

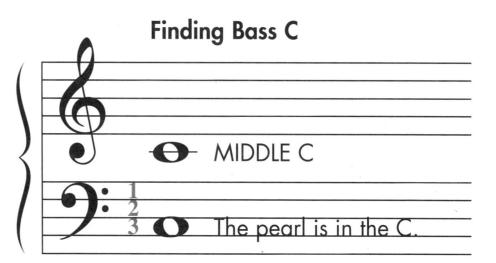

Finding Bass C

MIDDLE C

The pearl is in the C.

36 Pearl in the C

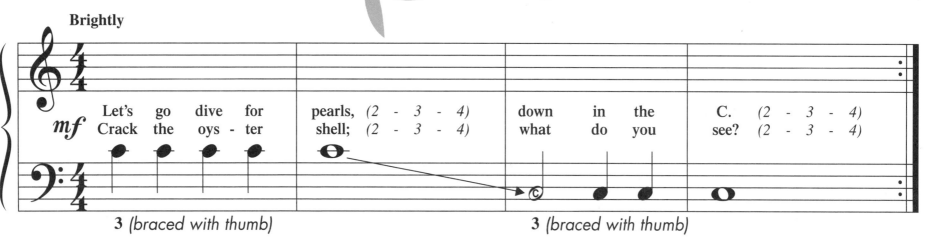

Brightly

mf

| Let's | go | dive | for | pearls, | (2 - 3 - 4) | down | in | the | C. | (2 - 3 - 4) |
| Crack | the | oys - | ter | shell; | (2 - 3 - 4) | what | do | you | see? | (2 - 3 - 4) |

3 *(braced with thumb)*   3 *(braced with thumb)*

The Octave

1. From one C to the next C is **8** white keys.
   This is called an **octave**. Say this word aloud.

2. Your teacher will help you find other octaves.

3. Now play the piece. Brace finger 3's with the thumbs!

37 ## Octave Blues

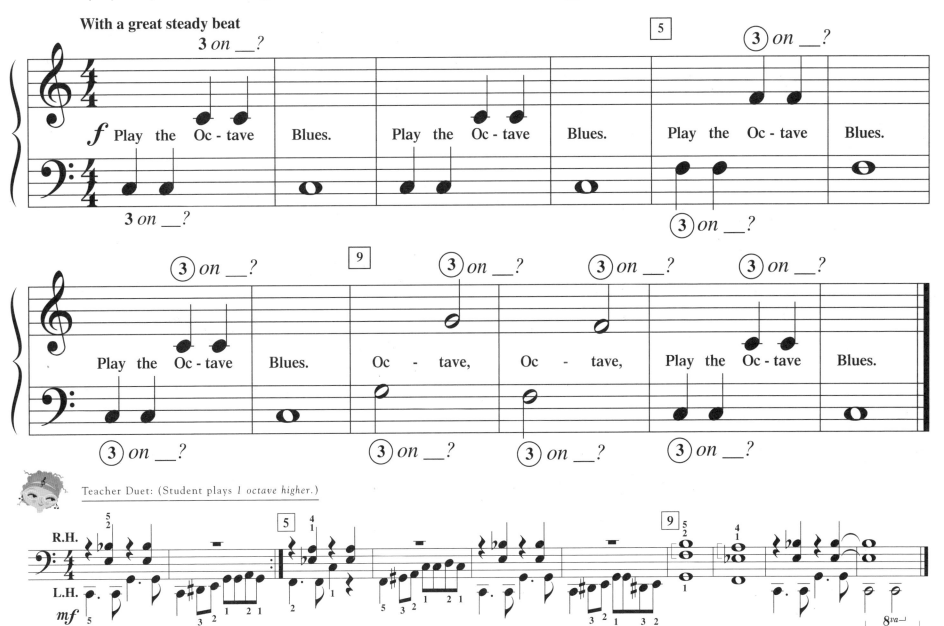

Teacher Duet: (Student plays *1 octave higher.*)

C 5-Finger Scale on the Bass Staff

In music, a scale is like a ladder that steps
UP and DOWN from one key to the next.

1. Point to each note and say LINE or SPACE.

2. Now, your teacher will read each clue to you.
   Say and play the answer on the keyboard.

C	D	E	F	G
space	*line*	*space*	*line*	*space*

Clues:

C — 1 - 2 - 3.
The pearl is in
the _____.

D — Hey, diddle, diddle,
what's in the
middle? _____

E — Hey, diddle D,
step up to _____.

F — In the bass clef,
line 2 is _____?

G — A is the top
line, STEP down
to _____?

38 This Is My C Scale

Steady march tempo

mf This is my C | scale. *(2 - 3 - 4)* | This is my C | scale. *(2 - 3 - 4)*

The stem
on Bass C
goes UP.

5   1   1   5

FF1621

5

This is my C scale. *(2 - 3 - 4)* This is my C scale. *(2 - 3 - 4)*

9 *(Optional: Hands together)*

This is my C scale. *(2 - 3 - 4)* This is my C scale. *(2 - 3 - 4)*

Teacher Duet: (Student plays *as written*.)

D I S C O V E R Y Can you name the notes of the **C 5-finger scale** forward and backward?

♩ Also, anybody see Tap?

FF1621

69

Tips from the Dragon:

1. Write the starting note for each hand in the marshmallows below.

2. Can you play without looking at your hands?

39 Pet Dragon

Name the 5-finger scale. _____

Words by Crystal Bowman

Strutting along

R.H.

f I have a pet drag-on, he's the best pet in my town.
He heats spa-ghet-ti and makes such hot, de-li-cious toast.

L.H.

1 Think: A is the top line. Step down to _____ ?

He's my bud-dy and my pal, he fol-lows me a-round.
He comes in quite hand-y at a big marsh-mal-low roast.

Teacher Duet: (Student plays *1 octave higher.*)

R.H.

L.H. *mf*

Fine

Tip from Carlos:

Read the *up* and *down* direction of the noteheads!

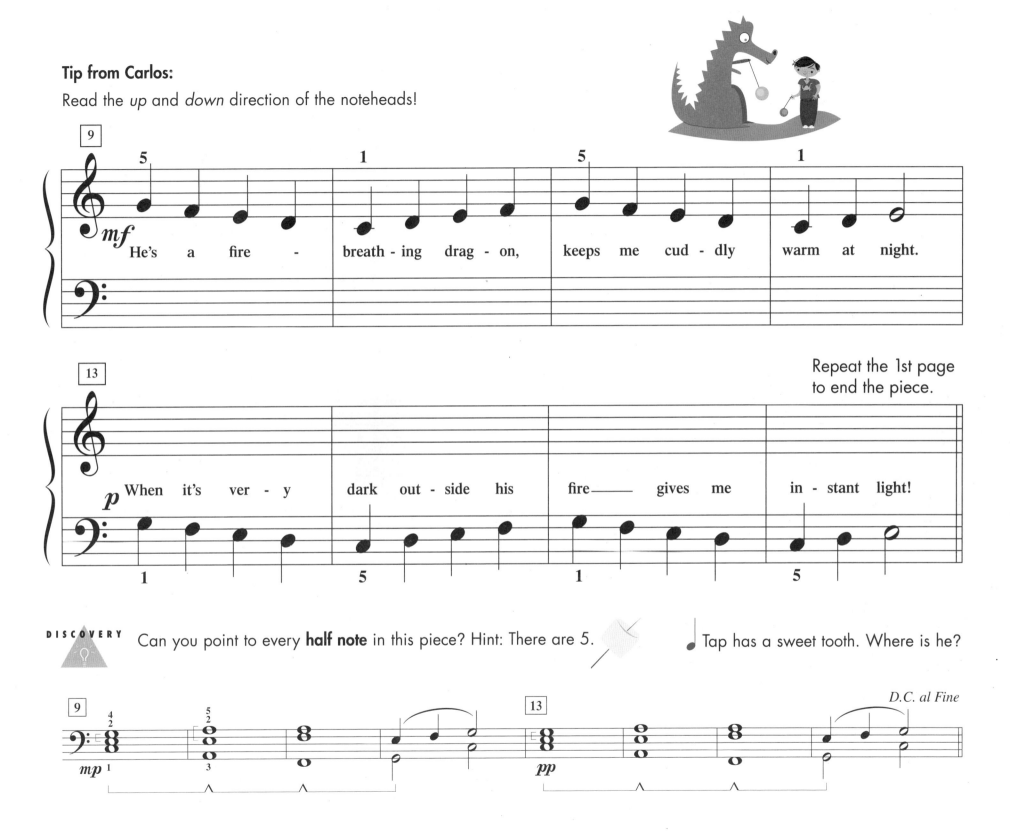

9

mf
He's   a   fire - breath - ing   drag - on,   keeps   me   cud - dly   warm   at   night.

13

Repeat the 1st page
to end the piece.

p When   it's   ver - y   dark   out - side   his   fire——— gives   me   in - stant   light!

DISCOVERY Can you point to every **half note** in this piece? Hint: There are 5.   ♩ Tap has a sweet tooth. Where is he?

9   *D.C. al Fine*

mp   **13**   *pp*

A Note from Mozart:

My sister Nannerl and I loved to play Hide-and-Seek.
Help Nannerl hide by playing "thumb whispers."

Thumb Whispers:

1. Tap your L.H. thumb quickly and lightly *8 times* on your
   • head   • shoulder   • knee

At the keyboard:

2. Play and notice the *f* and *p* signs.

3. Use a "whisper thumb" at *measures 5-7*.

40 Hide-and-Seek

Wolfgang Amadeus Mozart
(from Sonata for Four Hands, K19d)

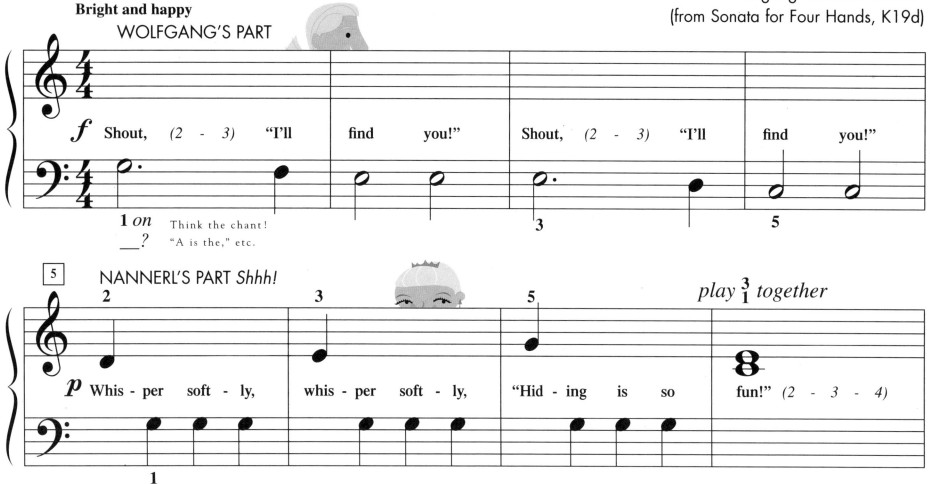

Bright and happy

WOLFGANG'S PART

f Shout, (2 - 3) "I'll find you!" Shout, (2 - 3) "I'll find you!"

1 *on*
__? Think the chant! "A is the," etc.

3   5

NANNERL'S PART *Shhh!*

play 3/1 together

p Whis - per soft - ly, whis - per soft - ly, "Hid - ing is so fun!" (2 - 3 - 4)

WOLFGANG'S PART

9

f Shout, *(2 - 3)* "I'll find you!" Shout, *(2 - 3)* "I'll find you!"

NANNERL'S PART *Shhh!*

13

p Whis - per soft - ly, "Don't laugh, qui - et, here he comes!"

DISCOVERY
Your teacher will play *measures 5–8* and somewhere *BUMP* the L.H. thumb.
Stop your teacher and tell him/her how to correct the sound!
HINT: Tell your teacher to play on the side tip.

Teacher Duet: (Student plays *1 octave higher.*)

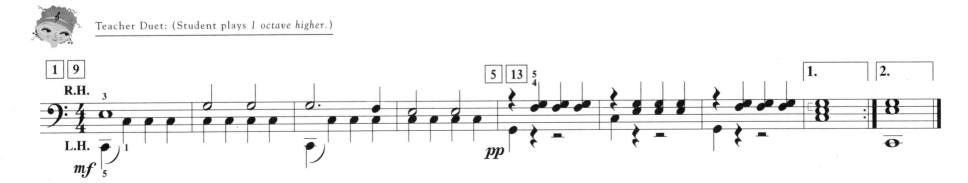

The Tie

A **tie** is a curved line connecting 2 notes on the *SAME* line or space.
The note will be played *once* but held for the length of both notes combined.

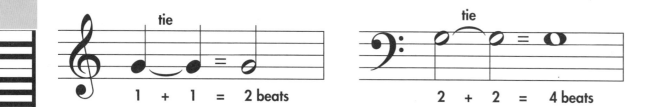

1 + 1 = 2 beats

2 + 2 = 4 beats

Hot Chocolate, Whipped-Cream Day

41

Words by Crystal Bowman

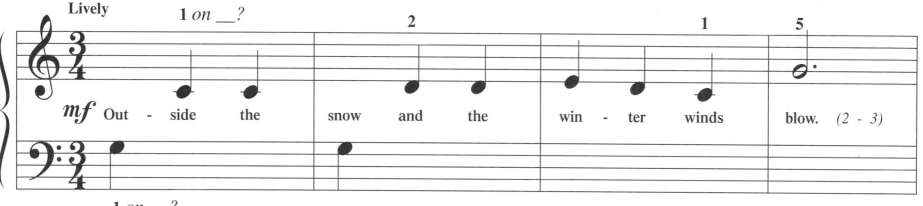

Lively

1 *on* __?

mf Out - side the snow and the win - ter winds blow. *(2 - 3)*

1 *on* __?   Think the chant! "A is the," etc.

Teacher Duet: (Student plays *1 octave higher.*)

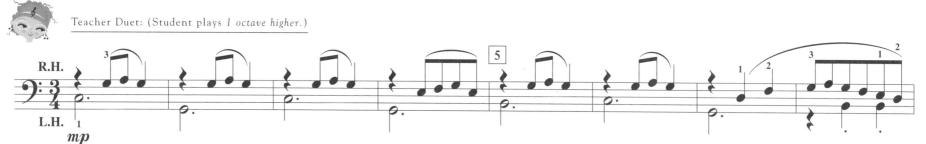

R.H.

L.H.

mp

Out - side there're moun - tains of snow. *(2 - 3 - 1 - 2 - 3)*

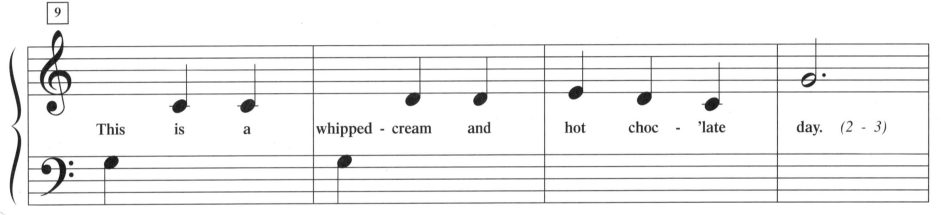

This is a whipped - cream and hot choc - 'late day. *(2 - 3)*

In - side is where I will stay. *(2 - 3 - 1 - 2 - 3)*

Tips from the lark:

1. Write the *bottom* L.H. note in the bird feather below.
   Hint: Say the rhyme from page 66:
   1-2-3. The pearl is in the _____ ?

2. Try playing the song very high on
   the keyboard where a lark might sing!

Alouette

Name the 5-finger scale. _____

French Folk Song

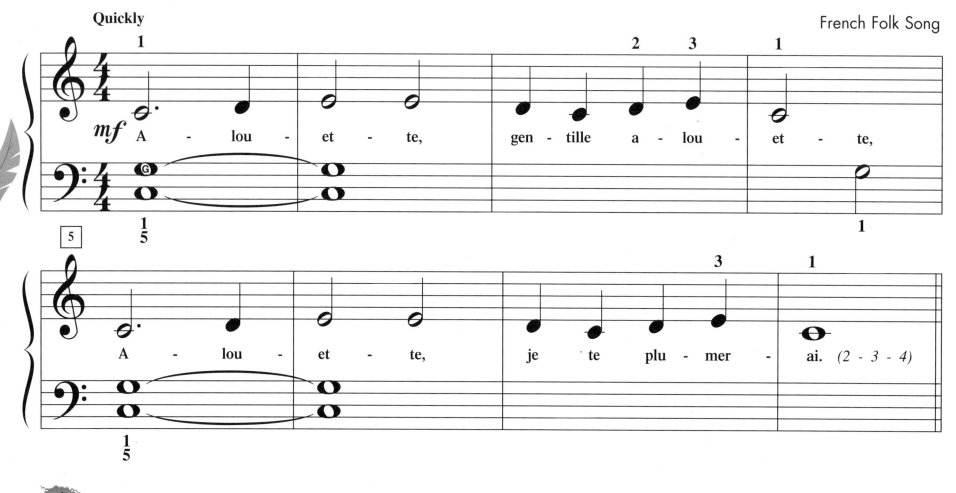

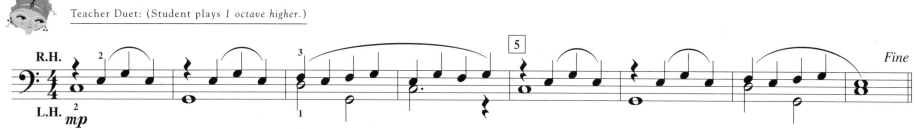

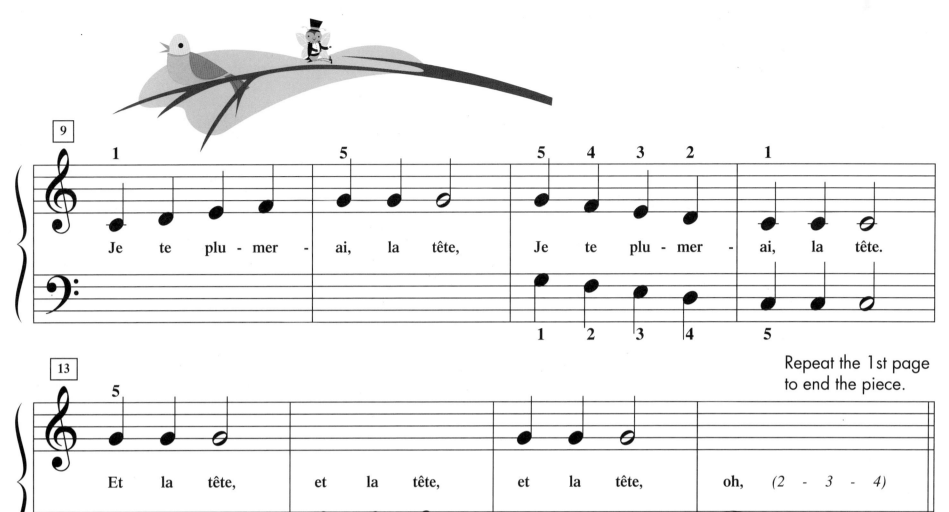

Repeat the 1st page
to end the piece.

DISCOVERY Can you play this piece from memory?

Mrs. Razzle-Dazzle's cat Mitsy sometimes disappears at night. Where do you think she goes?

Tips from Mitsy:

1. Sing the melody on "la" with the CD to *FEEL* the rhythm.

2. Name each L.H. note. Do you see a pattern?

3. Play and have fun!

Alley Cat Choir

Words by Crystal Bowman

Happily

1 on __?

2 on __?

mf Ear - ly in the eve - ning when the sun goes down,
Kit - ty tails are sing - in' and they're meow - in' low,

Teacher Duet: (Student plays *1 octave higher*.)

The Quarter Rest

Music often has moments of silence called **rests**.

quarter rest 𝄽 means *silence* for 1 beat

Tips from Ludwig:

1. Tap the rhythm below and count aloud.

2. Hint: Whisper the word *rest* as you make a quick, loose fist.

1   rest   1   rest   1 - 2 - 3   1   1   rest   1   1   1 - 2 - 3 - 4

44 # Write, Beethoven

(Symphony No. 5, Fourth Movement)

Lively

1   3   5   5   1

f Write,   write,   write *(2 - 3)*   a   sym-pho-ny   to-   night. Now it's   done.   The   End!

Prepare **L.H. finger 3** on the LOWEST C.

Play the LOWEST C.

Tips from Katie:

1. Tap and count the rhythm with your teacher:
   1 *rest* **1 1**, etc.

   Make a loose fist as you whisper "rest."

2. Now play with a steady beat. **Feel** the rest!

45

Rock It and Roll It

Name the 5-finger scale. _____

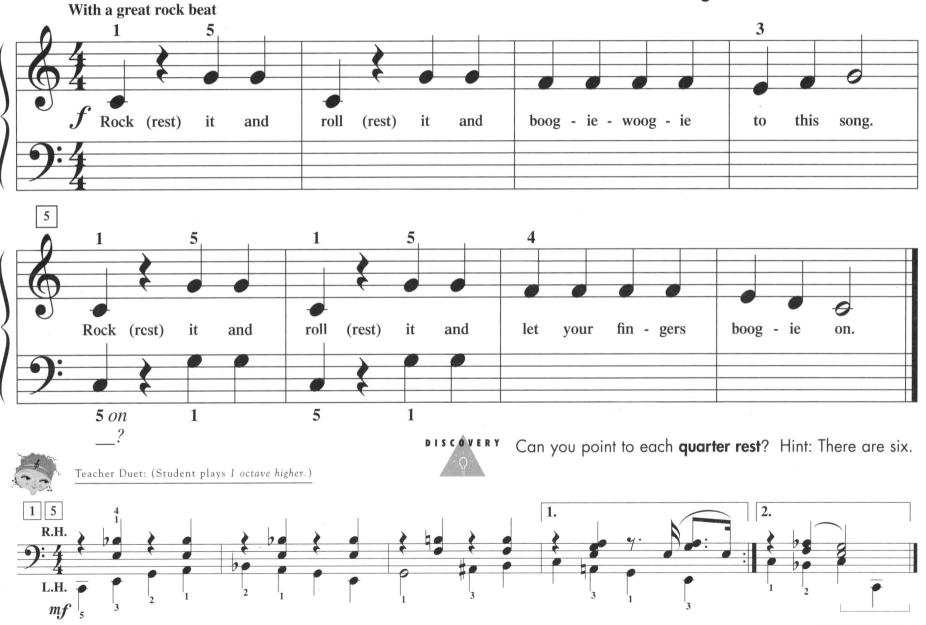

With a great rock beat

Rock (rest) it and roll (rest) it and boog - ie - woog - ie to this song.

Rock (rest) it and roll (rest) it and let your fin - gers boog - ie on.

5 on ___?

DISCOVERY Can you point to each **quarter rest**? Hint: There are six.

Teacher Duet: (Student plays *1 octave higher.*)

F1621

WRITING BOOK 60-61

Star Crossing Over: (on the closed keyboard)

1. Balance your **R.H.** on all five fingertips.
   Pretend this is Tap's home at night.

2. **L.H. finger 2** is the star. Lift it over "Tap's house" and set it
   down just *above* R.H. finger 5.

3. Now bring your L.H. back to a round hand shape.
   Repeat several times.

At the keyboard:

4. Play and enjoy your fine piano technique.
   Have fun with the duets!

TECHNIQUE GAME: Star Crossing Over

Twinkle, Twinkle Little Star
Theme and Variations

(based on Mozart's Piano Variations,
Ah! vous dirai-je, Maman)

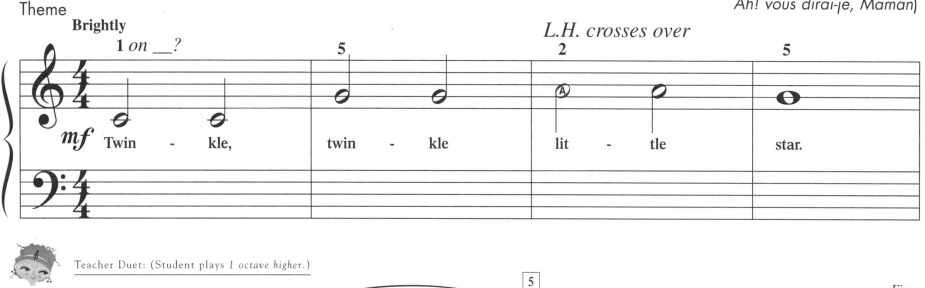

Theme

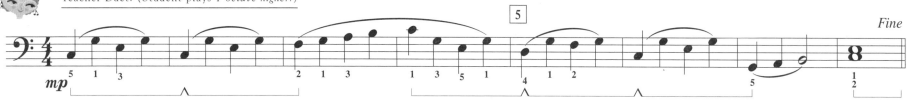

Teacher Duet: (Student plays *1 octave higher*.)

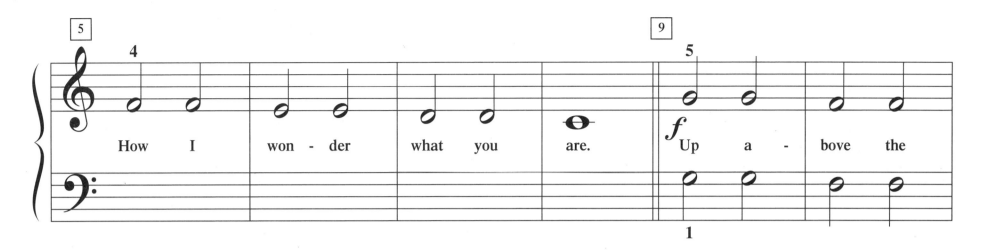

How I | won - der | what you | are. | *f* Up a - | bove the

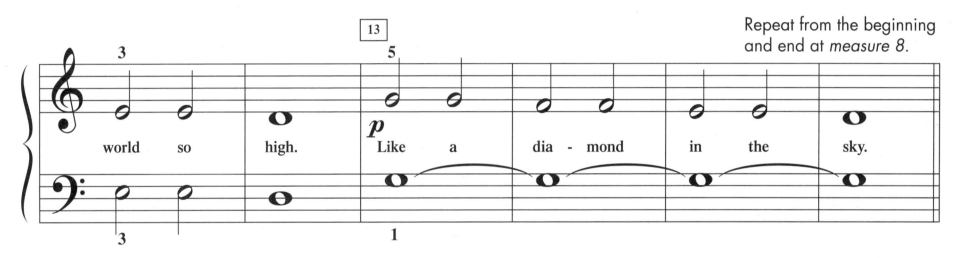

world so | high. | *p* Like a | dia - mond | in the | sky.

Repeat from the beginning
and end at *measure 8.*

CREATIVE After you have learned **Variation 1** and **2**, can you make up your own variation?
Try changing the dynamics, the rhythm, the tempo (speed), or a few notes!

♩ Where's Tap?

D.C. al Fine

Twinkle, Twinkle Variation 1

47

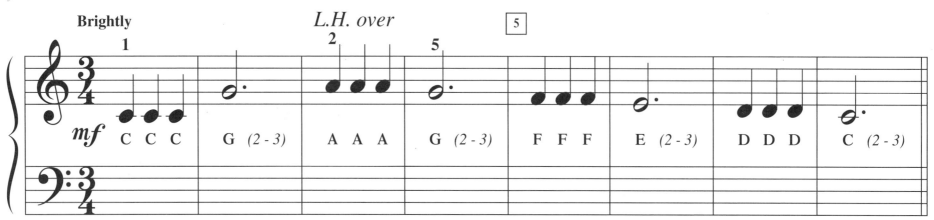

Repeat from the beginning
and end at *measure 8.*

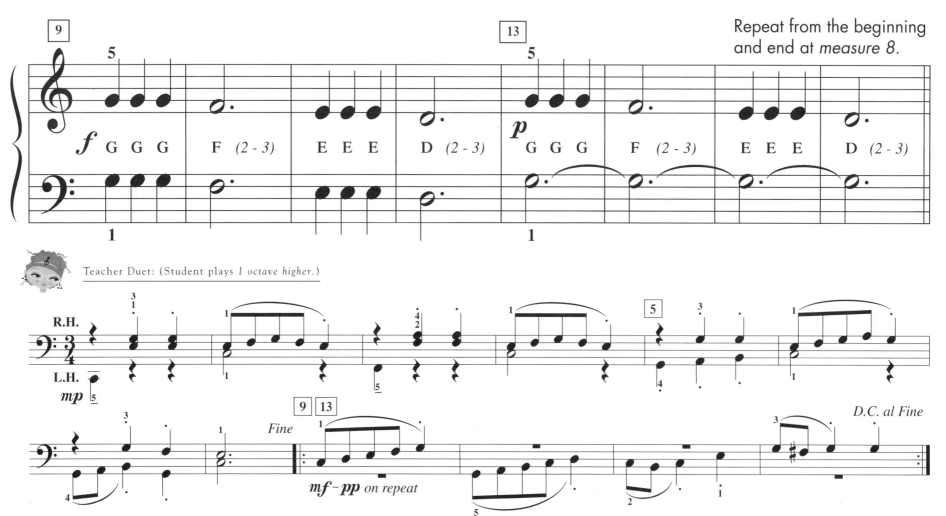

Teacher Duet: (Student plays *1 octave higher.*)

Twinkle, Twinkle Variation 2

Brightly

L.H. over

Repeat from the beginning and end at *measure 8.*

Teacher Duet: (Student plays *1 octave higher.*)

ped. simile

Fine

mf–pp on repeat

D.C. al Fine

Music Library
Dictionary

Your teacher may ask you for information about each book.
For example, "Can you tell me about a bar line?"

Have fun being the music librarian!

bar line
A short line that creates a measure.

bass C
3rd space down
"1-2-3. The pearl is in the C."

bass clef
Shows notes below Middle C.
Also known as the F clef.

bass F
2nd line down
(first F below Middle C)

C 5-Finger Scale
C-D-E-F-G
Five notes that step up from C.

dotted half note
3 beats
Count: 1-2-3

double bar line
The end of the piece.
(a thin and thick line)

duet
Two people playing at the same time.
(4 hands)

forte
The Italian word for loud.
Play firmly.

grand staff
R.H. uses the top staff.
L.H. uses the lower staff.

half note
2 beats
Count: 1-2

improvise
Making up music "on the spot."

measure
Musical beats are grouped into measures.

mezzo forte
The Italian word for moderately loud.

Middle C
Middle C is on a short line between the staffs.

octave — 8 notes from Middle C to Bass C is an octave.

piano — The Italian word for soft. *p* Play gently.

primo — The higher part of a 4-hand duet.

quarter note — 1 beat. Count: 1

repeat sign — Play once again.

rest — Silence for 1 beat.

secondo — The lower part of a 4-hand duet.

staff — 5 lines and 4 spaces.

step — line to space or space to line

tempo — The speed of the music.

tie — A curved line connecting the same notes. Hold for the total counts of both.

time signature — 4/4 beats in a measure ♩ gets 1 beat

time signature — 3/4 beats in a measure ♩ gets 1 beat

treble clef — Shows notes above Middle C. Also known as the G clef.

treble G — 2nd line up (first G above Middle C)

whole note — 4 beats. Count: 1-2-3-4

Congratulations, my friend

Sign and join the club!
Can you name each friend?

You have completed
My First Piano Adventure® Lesson Book B.
We can't wait to see you in Lesson Book C!